OLD MOORE'S

HOROSCOPE AND ASTRAL DIARY

SCORPIO

OLD MOORE'S

HOROSCOPE AND ASTRAL DIARY

SCORPIO

foulsham

LONDON • NEW YORK • TORONTO • SYDNEY

foulsham

The Old Barrel Store, Drayman's Lane, Marlow, Bucks SL7 2FF

Foulsham books can be found in all good bookshops and direct from
www.foulsham.com

ISBN: 978-0-572-04499-2

Copyright © 2014 W. Foulsham & Co. Ltd

A CIP record for this book is available from the British Library

Typeset in Great Britain by Chris Brewer Origination, Christchurch
Printed in Great Britain by Martins The Printers, Berwick-upon-Tweed

CONTENTS

INTRODUCTION

Astrology has been a part of life for centuries now, and no matter how technological our lives become, it seems that it never diminishes in popularity. For thousands of years people have been gazing up at the star-clad heavens and seeing their own activities and proclivities reflected in the movement of those little points of light. Across centuries countless hours have been spent studying the way our natures, activities and decisions seem to be paralleled by their predictable movements. Old Moore, a time-served veteran in astrological research, continues to monitor the zodiac and has produced the Astral Diary for 2015, tailor-made to your own astrological makeup.

Old Moore's Astral Diary is unique in its ability to get the heart of your nature and to offer you the sort of advice that might come from a trusted friend. It enables you to see in a day-by-day sense exactly how the planets are working for you. The diary section advises how you can get the best from upcoming situations and allows you to plan ahead successfully. There's also room on each daily entry to record your own observations or appointments.

While other popular astrology books merely deal with your astrological 'Sun sign', the Astral Diaries go much further. Every person on the planet is unique and Old Moore allows you to access your individuality in a number of ways. The front section gives you the chance to work out the placement of the Moon at the time of your birth and to see how its position has set an important seal on your overall nature. Perhaps most important of all, you can use the Astral Diary to discover your Rising Sign. This is the zodiac sign that was appearing over the Eastern horizon at the time of your birth and is just as important to you as an individual as is your Sun sign.

It is the synthesis of many different astrological possibilities that makes you what you are and with the Astral Diaries you can learn so much. How do you react to love and romance? Through the unique Venus tables and the readings that follow them, you can learn where the planet Venus was at the time of your birth. It is even possible to register when little Mercury is 'retrograde', which means that it appears to be moving backwards in space when viewed from the Earth. Mercury rules communication, so be prepared to deal with a few setbacks in this area when you see the sign ☿. The Astral Diary will be an interest and a support throughout the whole year ahead.

Old Moore extends his customary greeting to all people of the Earth and offers his age-old wishes for a happy and prosperous period ahead.

THE ESSENCE OF SCORPIO

Exploring the Personality of
Scorpio the Scorpion

(24TH OCTOBER – 22ND NOVEMBER)

What's in a sign?

To say that you are a little complicated and somewhat difficult to understand is probably a great understatement. The basic reason for this lies in the peculiar nature of Scorpio rulership. In terms of the elements, your zodiac sign is a Water sign. This makes you naturally emotional, deep, somewhat reserved and ever anxious to help those around you. As a direct contrast, classical astrologers always maintained that your planetary ruler was Mars. Mars is the planet of combat and aggression, being positive and dominant under most circumstances. So it can be judged from the start that there are great contradictions within the basic Scorpio nature.

It's a fact that many people are naturally cautious of Scorpio people. Perhaps this isn't surprising. Under most circumstances you appear to be quiet and peaceful, but the situation is a little like a smoking bomb. When it comes to defending yourself, or in particular those people who you see as being important to you, there is virtually no limit to which you would refuse to go. Generally speaking our ancient ancestors were extremely wise in terms of the names they gave to the different zodiac signs. Consider the apparently diminutive and retiring scorpion. It doesn't go looking for trouble and is generally happy to remain in the shadows. However, if it is provoked, or even attacked, it will take on adversaries many times its own size. It carries a barbed sting in its tail and will strike without any additional warning if necessary.

All the same, the Scorpio reputation may be a little undeserved. Yours is one of the most compassionate and caring of all the zodiac signs. When it comes to working on behalf of humanity, especially the oppressed, the sick or the disenfranchised, you show your true mettle.

You cannot stand the thought of people suffering unjustifiably, which is why many of the great social reformers and even freedom fighters had the same zodiac sign as you do.

As a Scorpio you are likely to be intuitive (some would say psychic) and under most circumstances you are more than willing to follow that little voice inside yourself that tells you how to behave in any given situation.

Scorpio resources

Your nature is so very often understated that it might be said that your greatest resource is surprise. You have the ability to shock people constantly, even those who think they understand you perfectly well. This brings us back to the creature for which your zodiac sign is named. A scorpion is diminutive – and would represent a tasty snack for any would-be predator. However, it defies logic by standing its ground and fighting back. When it does, woe betide the aggressor that refuses to take account of its presence. And so it is with you. Quiet, even reserved, you tend to get on with your work. This you do efficiently and without undue fuss, approaching each task with the same methodical attitude. People often don't even realise that you are around. And then, when they least expect it, there you are!

The ability to surprise means that you often get on in life against heavy odds. In addition you have great resilience and fortitude. It is possible for you to continue to work long and hard under circumstances that would force others to retreat. Most Scorpio people would not consider themselves to be tough – in fact quite a few are positively neurotic when it comes to matters associated with their own health. Yet you can endure hardship well and almost always win through in the end.

It's true that you may not be quite as confident as you could be. If you were, people would notice you more and that would detract from that all-important element of surprise that makes you so formidable, and which is definitely the most important weapon in your armoury. However, it is clear that your greatest resource is compassion, and on those occasions when you really allow it to show, you display yourself as being one of the most important allies to your fellow men and women.

At a practical level you are more than capable and can often be expected to perform tasks that you haven't necessarily undertaken before. You have a deep intelligence and good powers to reason things out. Most important of all is a determination that no other zodiac sign can match.

Beneath the surface

This section of an account of the typical Scorpio nature could fill an entire book in itself because you are such a complicated person. However, there are certain advantages to being a Scorpio. For example, nobody is going to run away with the idea that you are basically uncomplicated and shallow. It ought to be clear enough to the dullest observer that there is a boiling, seething volcano bubbling away beneath the surface of almost every Scorpio subject.

You are often accused of having a slightly dark view of life, and it's true that many Scorpio people enjoy a rather morbid curiosity and are fascinated by subjects that make other people shudder. At the same time you could hardly be described as being one of life's natural optimists. Part of the reason for this lies in the fact that you have been disappointed in the past and may have arrived at the conclusion that to expect the worst is often the most sensible course of action. At least that way you are likely to mitigate some of the potential depression regarding failures in the future.

Although this way of thinking is somewhat faulty, it comes so naturally to the Scorpio subject that it actually works very well, though it has to be said that it might be responsible for a tendency to hold back on occasions. Assessing the way your inner mind works is as difficult for you as it is for any outsider. Even individuals who have been friends for years will sometimes come desperately unstuck if they arrive at the conclusion that they know well what makes you tick. In the recesses of your mind you are passionate, driving, restless, dissatisfied and frequently disappointed with your own efforts. On the other hand, you have the power to make dreams into realities and are excellent at hatching plans that will benefit people far from your own circle and circumstances. Being a tireless worker on behalf of the oppressed, the fate of humanity as a whole is ever an inner concern.

When you love you do so with great width and depth. Your capacity for jealousy knows no bounds and there are times when you can be as destructive to yourself as you ever could be regarding any other individual. Yet for all this your inner mind is lofty and can soar like an eagle on occasions. If the world at large was able to fathom just one tenth of the way your inner mind actually works, people would find you even more fascinating than they do already. But perhaps it's best that they don't. The deepest recesses of Scorpio are an intense secret and will usually stay that way.

Making the best of yourself

It isn't hard to find a single word that describes the way you can make the best of yourself, especially when viewed by the world at large. That word is 'communication'. When difficulties arise in your life, especially concerning other people, it's usually because you haven't managed to get your message across, and probably because you haven't even tried to do so. There is much to your nature that is electric, powerful and magnetic. These qualities make you potentially popular and fascinating to a wealth of individuals. Hide these qualities beneath too brusque an exterior and you can seem dark and brooding.

Of course it's a fine line and one that isn't easy to walk. You are constantly worried that if you show people what really makes you tick, they will not find you interesting at all. In reality this concern is totally without foundation. There is more than enough depth about you to last several lifetimes. It doesn't matter how much you give of yourself to the world at large, there are always going to be surprises galore to follow.

Use the dynamic qualities of your nature to the full. Traditionally your ruling planet is Mars – a real go-getter of a planetary ruler and one that imbues you with tremendous power to get things done at a practical level. On the way you need to show how much you care about others. Amidst a plethora of gifts offered to you by the celestial spheres, your ability to help others is likely to be top of the list. When you are giving you are also usually approachable. For you the two go hand in hand. Avoid allowing yourself to become morose or inward looking and always strive to find simple answers to simple questions.

Stick to some sort of work that you find interesting. That can be almost anything to a Scorpio, as long as it feeds the inner you. It does need to carry a degree of diversity and should ideally have an end product that is easy to see. On your journey through life don't get carried away with daydreams – yet on the other hand avoid losing your great potential to make them come true.

The impressions you give

This is one area of your life over which you do have a great deal of control. If the adage 'what you see is what you get' turns out to be true for many signs of the zodiac, it certainly isn't the case with you. The complexity of your nature makes it difficult for even you to find 'the real Scorpio', and in any case this tends to change from day to day. However, regarding some matters there isn't any doubt at all. Firstly you are deeply magnetic and possess the ability to arouse an instinctive fascination in others. Ally this to your propensity for being very positive in your decision making and you have a potentially formidable combination.

Most people already think of you as being an extremely interesting person. Unfortunately they may also occasionally consider you to be a little cool and somewhat difficult to approach. Neither of these impressions are true, it's simply that you are quite shy at heart, and sometimes find it difficult to believe that you could be liked by certain individuals. Learn to throw this erroneous assumption out of the window, and instead, expect to be viewed positively. To do so would make all the difference and would clear the way so that your more personable side can show all the time.

Very few people who know you well could fail to realise that you care deeply, especially about the well-being of the oppressed. You have a truly noble spirit, a fact that shines through in practically everything you do – yet another reason to be noticed.

It's true that you can sometimes make your secretive quality into an art form, which those looking in from the outside might find rather difficult to deal with. This represents another outward aspect of your nature that could so easily be altered. By all means keep your secrets, though not about matters that are of no real note whatsoever. In a single phrase, try to lighten up a little. It's all you need to be almost perfect!

The way forward

It must first be held in mind that Scorpio people are complicated. That's something you simply cannot get away from, no matter how much you might try. On the one hand you can deal with practical matters almost instinctively. You are resourceful, deep thinking, intense and fascinating. On the other side of the coin you are often too fond of luxury and will frequently withdraw yourself from situations that you do not care to pursue. You can be quite stubborn and can even bear a grudge if you feel that you have been provoked.

It is suggested in astrology that no quality of nature is necessarily good or bad, it really depends on the way it is used. For example, stubbornness can be considered a terrible fault, but not if you were being awkward concerning the obvious rights of an oppressed person or group. It turns out that Scorpio has more of a potential to be 'saint or sinner' than any zodiac sign. As long as you examine your motives in any given situation, whilst at the same time trying to cultivate a degree of flexibility that is not one of your natural gifts, then you won't go far wrong.

Turn on the charm when it is necessary because it will rarely if ever let you down. Think about the way you can serve the world, but don't preach about it. Love sincerely, but don't allow jealousy to spoil things. Be constructive in your determination and don't get on your high horse when it isn't necessary. Follow these simple rules for the best chance of progress.

Of course there are many positives around to start with. You are a very loyal friend, are capable of being extremely brave and tend to be very committed to family members. At the same time you are trustworthy and can work long and hard using your own initiative. Although you sometimes worry about your health, you are more robust than most and can endure a high degree of hardship if necessary. You don't take kindly to criticism but can be flexible enough to accept it if you know it is intended for your own good.

Few people doubt your sincerity – that is, when they know what you believe. So it's important to lay your thoughts on the line right from the start. And even if you don't choose to treat the whole world as a friend, you are capable of gathering a little circle around you who would never let you down. Do make sure, however, that this 'inner group' isn't simply comprised of other Scorpios!

SCORPIO ON THE CUSP

Old Moore is often asked how astrological profiles are altered for those people born at either the beginning or the end of a zodiac sign, or, more properly, on the cusps of a sign. In the case of Scorpio this would be on the 24th of October and for two or three days after, and similarly at the end of the sign, probably from the 20th to the 22nd of November. In this year's Astral Diaries, once again, Old Moore sets out to explain the differences regarding cuspid signs.

The Libra Cusp – October 24th to 26th

You are probably generally considered to be a bright and breezy sort of character, with a great deal of enthusiasm for life. Despite this, few people would doubt that you are a shrewd operator, and that you know what you want and have a fairly good idea of how to go about getting it. Not everyone likes you as much as you would wish, but that's because the Libran side of your nature longs for popularity, while set against this is your deep Scorpio need to speak your mind, even when you know that other people might wish you did not indulge in this trait very frequently.

In love, you typify the split between these two signs. On the one hand you are passionate, sincere and intense, while on the other your Libran responses can cause a certain fickle sort of affection to show sometimes, probably to the confusion of those with whom you are involved at a personal level. Nevertheless, few people would find fault with your basic nature and there isn't much doubt that your heart is in the right place.

When it comes to career matters, you have a very fortunate combination. Scorpio can sometimes be accused of lacking diplomacy, but nothing could be further from the truth with Libra. As a result, you have what it takes in terms of determination but at the same time you are capable of seeing the point of view put forward by colleagues. You tend to rise to the top of the tree and, with your mixture of raw ability and humour that most of the world approves of, you can stay there.

You won't be the sort of person to make quite as many enemies as Scorpio taken alone might do, and you need the cut and thrust of the world much more than the retiring creature after whom your zodiac sign is named. Try not to be controversial and do your best to retain a sense of humour, which is essential to your well-being. Few would doubt the fact that your heart is in the right place and your creative potential could be second to none. Most important of all, you need the self-satisfaction that comes from living in the real world.

The Sagittarius Cusp – November 20th to 22nd

You can be a really zany character, with a love of life that is second to none. Add to this a penetrating insight, a razor-sharp wit and an instinctive intuition that is quite remarkable and we find in you a formidable person. It's true that not everyone understands what makes you tick, probably least of all yourself, but you strive to be liked and really do want to advertise your willingness to learn and to grow, which isn't always the province of Scorpio when taken alone. Your capacity for work knows no bounds, though you don't really like to get your hands dirty and would feel more content when telling others what to do.

In a career sense, you need to be in a position from which you are able to delegate. This is not because you are afraid of hard work yourself, far from it, but you possess a strong ability to see through problems and you are a natural director of others. Sales careers may interest you, or a position from which you can organise and arrange things. However, you hate to be tied down to one place for long, so you would be at your best when allowed to move around freely and do things in your own way.

You are a natural social reformer, mainly because you are sure that you know what is right and just. In the main you are correct in your assumptions, but there are occasions when you should realise that there is more than one form of truth. Perhaps you are not always quite as patient with certain individuals as you might be but these generally tend to be people who show traits of cruelty or cunning.

As a family person, you care very much for the people who figure most prominently in your life. Sometimes you are a definite home bird, with a preference for what you know and love, but this is offset by a restless trend within your nature that often sends you off into the wide blue yonder, chasing rainbows that the Scorpio side of your nature doubts are even there. Few would doubt your charm, your magnetism, or your desire to get ahead in life in almost any way possible. You combine patience with genuine talent and make a loyal, interesting and entertaining friend or lover.

SCORPIO AND ITS ASCENDANTS

The nature of every individual on the planet is composed of the rich variety of zodiac signs and planetary positions that were present at the time of their birth. Your Sun sign, which in your case is Scorpio, is one of the many factors when it comes to assessing the unique person you are. Probably the most important consideration, other than your Sun sign, is to establish the zodiac sign that was rising over the eastern horizon at the time that you were born. This is your Ascending or Rising sign. Most popular astrology fails to take account of the Ascendant, and yet its importance remains with you from the very moment of your birth, through every day of your life. The Ascendant is evident in the way you approach the world, and so, when meeting a person for the first time, it is this astrological influence that you are most likely to notice first. Our Ascending sign essentially represents what we appear to be, while the Sun sign is what we feel inside ourselves.

The Ascendant also has the potential for modifying our overall nature. For example, if you were born at a time of day when Scorpio was passing over the eastern horizon (this would be around the time of dawn) then you would be classed as a double Scorpio. As such, you would typify this zodiac sign, both internally and in your dealings with others. However, if your Ascendant sign turned out to be a Fire sign, such as Aries, there would be a profound alteration of nature, away from the expected qualities of Scorpio.

One of the reasons why popular astrology often ignores the Ascendant is that it has always been rather difficult to establish. Old Moore has found a way to make this possible by devising an easy-to-use table, which you will find on page 125 of this book. Using this, you can establish your Ascendant sign at a glance. You will need to know your rough time of birth, then it is simply a case of following the instructions.

For those readers who have no idea of their time of birth it might be worth allowing a good friend, or perhaps your partner, to read through the section that follows this introduction. Someone who deals with you on a regular basis may easily discover your Ascending sign, even though you could have some difficulty establishing it for yourself. A good understanding of this component of your nature is essential if you want to be aware of that 'other person' who is responsible for the way you make contact with the world at large. Your Sun sign, Ascendant sign, and the other pointers in this book will, together, allow you a far better understanding of what makes you tick as an individual. Peeling back the different layers of your astrological make-up can be an enlightening experience, and the Ascendant may represent one of the most important layers of all.

Scorpio with Scorpio Ascendant

This is one of the most potent of all astrological possibilities, but how it is used depends so very much on the individual who possesses it. On the one hand you are magnetic, alluring, sexy, deep and very attractive, whilst at the same time you are capable of being stubborn, self-seeking, vain, over-sensitive and fathomless. It has to be said that under most circumstances the first set of adjectives are the most appropriate, and that is because you keep control of the deeper side, refusing to allow it absolute control over your conscious life. You are able to get almost anything you want from life, but first you have to discover what that might be. The most important factor of all, however, is the way you can offer yourself, totally and without reservation to a needy world.

Self-sacrifice is a marvellous thing, but you can go too far on occasions. The furthest extreme for Scorpios here is a life that is totally dedicated to work and prayer. For the few this is admirable, for the still earth-based, less so. Finding a compromise is not easy as you are not always in touch with yourself. Feed the spiritual, curb the excesses, accept the need for luxury, and be happy.

Scorpio with Sagittarius Ascendant

There are many gains with this combination, and most of you reading this will already be familiar with the majority of them. Sagittarius offers a bright and hopeful approach to life, but may not always have the staying power and the patience to get what it really needs. Scorpio, on the other hand, can be too deep for its own good, is very self-seeking on occasions and extremely giving to others. Both the signs have problems when taken on their own, and, it has to be said, double the difficulties when they come together. But this is not usually the case. Invariably the presence of Scorpio slows down the over-quick responses of the Archer, whilst the inclusion of Sagittarius prevents Scorpio from taking itself too seriously.

Life is so often a game of extremes, when all the great spiritual masters of humanity have indicated that a 'middle way' is the path to choose. You have just the right combination of skills and mental faculties to find that elusive path, and can bring great joy to yourself and others as a result. Most of the time you are happy, optimistic, helpful and a joy to know. You have mental agility, backed up by a stunning intuition, which itself would rarely let you down. Keep a sense of proportion and understand that your depth of intellect is necessary to curb your flighty side.

Scorpio with Capricorn Ascendant

If patience, perseverance and a solid ability to get where you want to go are considered to be the chief components of a happy life, then you should be skipping about every day. Unfortunately this is not always the case and here we have two zodiac signs, both of which can be too deep for their own good. Both Scorpio and Capricorn are inclined to take themselves rather too seriously and your main lesson in life, and some would say the reason you have adopted this zodiac combination, is to 'lighten up'. If all that determination is pushed in the direction of your service to the world at large, you are seen as being one of the kindest people imaginable. This is really the only option for you, because if you turn this tremendous potential power inwards all the time you will become brooding, secretive and sometimes even selfish. Your eyes should be turned towards a needy humanity, which can be served with the dry but definite wit of Capricorn and the true compassion of Scorpio.

It is impossible with this combination to indicate what areas of life suit you the best. Certainly you adore luxury in all its forms, and yet you can get by with almost nothing. You desire travel, and at the same time love the comforts and stability of home. The people who know you best are aware that you are rather special. Listen to what they say.

Scorpio with Aquarius Ascendant

Here we have a combination that shows much promise and a flexibility that allows many changes in direction, allied to a power to succeed, sometimes very much against all the odds. Aquarius lightens the load of the Scorpio mind, turning the depths into potential and making intuitive foresight into a means for getting on in life. There are depths here, because even airy Aquarius isn't too easy to understand, and it is therefore a fact that some people with this combination will always be something of a mystery. However, even this fact can be turned to your advantage because it means that people will always be looking at you. Confidence is so often the key to success in life and the Scorpio–Aquarius mix offers this, or at least appears to do so. Even when this is not entirely the case, the fact that everyone around you believes it to be true is often enough.

You are usually good to know, and show a keen intellect and a deep intelligence, aided by a fascination for life that knows no bounds. When at your best you are giving, understanding, balanced and active. On those occasions when things are not going well for you, beware a stubborn streak and the need to be sensational. Keep it light and happy and you won't go far wrong. Most of you are very, very well loved.

Scorpio with Pisces Ascendant

You stand a chance of disappearing so deep into yourself that other people would need one of those long ladders that cave explorers use, just to find you. It isn't really your fault because both Scorpio and Pisces are Water signs, which are difficult to understand, and you have them both. But that doesn't mean that you should be content to remain in the dark, and the warmth of your nature is all you need to shine a light on the wonderful qualities you possess. But the primary word of warning is that you must put yourself on display and allow others to know what you are, before their appreciation of these facts becomes apparent.

As a server of the world you are second to none and it is hard to find a person with this combination who is not, in some way, looking out for the people around them. Immensely attractive to others, you are also one of the most sought-after lovers. Much of this has to do with your deep and abiding charm, but the air of mystery that surrounds you also helps. Some of you will marry too early, and end up regretting the fact, though the majority of people with Scorpio and Pisces will find the love they deserve in the end. You are able, just, firm but fair, though a sucker for a hard luck story and as kind as the day is long. It's hard to imagine how so many good points could be ignored by others.

Scorpio with Aries Ascendant

The two very different faces of Mars come together in this potent, magnetic and quite awe-inspiring combination. Your natural inclination is towards secrecy, and this fact, together with the natural attractions of the sensual Scorpio nature, makes you the object of great curiosity. This means that you will not go short of attention and should ensure that you are always being analysed by people who may never get to know you at all. At heart you prefer your own company, and yet life appears to find means to push you into the public gaze time and again. Most people with this combination ooze sex appeal and can use this fact as a stepping stone to personal success, yet without losing any integrity or loosening the cords of a deeply moralistic nature.

On those occasions when you do lose your temper, there isn't a character in the length and breadth of the zodiac who would have either the words or the courage to stand against the stream of invective that follows. On really rare occasions you might even scare yourself. A simple look is enough to show family members when you are not amused. Few people are left unmoved by your presence in their life.

Scorpio with Taurus Ascendant

The first, last and most important piece of advice for you is not to take yourself, or anyone else, too seriously. This might be rather a tall order because Scorpio intensifies the deeper qualities of Taurus and can make you rather lacking in the sense of humour that we all need to live our lives in this most imperfect of worlds. You are naturally sensual by nature. This shows itself in a host of ways. In all probability you can spend hours in the bath, love to treat yourself to good food and drink and take your greatest pleasure in neat and orderly surroundings. This can often alienate you from those who live in the same house because other people need to use the bathroom from time to time and they cannot remain tidy indefinitely.

You tend to worry a great deal about things which are really not too important, but don't take this statement too seriously or you will begin to worry about this fact too! You often need to lighten up and should always do your best to tell yourself that most things are not half so important as they seem to be. Be careful over the selection of a life partner and if possible choose someone who is naturally funny and who does not take life anywhere near as seriously as you are inclined to do. At work you are more than capable and in all probability everyone relies heavily on your wise judgements.

Scorpio with Gemini Ascendant

What you are and what you appear to be can be two entirely different things with this combination. Although you appear to be every bit as chatty and even as flighty as Gemini tends to be, nothing could be further from the truth. In reality you have many deep and penetrating insights, all of which are geared towards sorting out potential problems before they come along. Few people would have the ability to pull the wool over your eyes, and you show a much more astute face to the world than is often the case for Gemini taken on its own. The level of your confidence, although not earth-shattering, is much greater with this combination, and you would not be thwarted once you had made up your mind.

There is a slight danger here, however, because Gemini is always inclined to nerve problems of one sort or another. In the main these are slight and fleeting, though the presence of Scorpio can intensify reactions and heighten the possibility of depression, which would not be at all fortunate. The best way round this potential problem is to have a wealth of friends, plenty to do and the sort of variety in your life that suits your Mercury ruler. Financial success is not too difficult to achieve because you can easily earn money and then manage to hold on to it.

Scorpio with Cancer Ascendant

There are few more endearing zodiac combinations than this one. Both signs are Watery in nature and show a desire to work on behalf of humanity as a whole. The world sees you as being genuinely caring, full of sympathy for anyone in trouble and always ready to lend a hand when it is needed. You are a loyal friend, a great supporter of the oppressed and a lover of home and family. In a work sense you are capable, and command respect from your colleagues, even though this comes about courtesy of your quiet competence and not as a result of anything that you might happen to say.

But we should not get too carried away with external factors, or the way that others see you. Inside you are a boiling pool of emotion.

You feel more strongly, love more deeply and hurt more fully than any other combination of the Water signs. Even those who think they know you really well would get a shock if they could take a stroll around the deeper recesses of your mind. Although these facts are true, they may be rather beside the point because it is a fact that the truth of your passion, commitment and deep convictions may only surface fully half a dozen times in your life. The fact is that you are a very private person at heart and you don't know how to be any other way.

Scorpio with Leo Ascendant

A Leo with intensity, that's what you are. You are mad about good causes and would argue the hind leg off a donkey in defence of your many ideals. If you are not out there saving the planet you could just be at home in the bath, thinking up the next way to save humanity from its own worst excesses. In your own life, although you love little luxuries, you are sparing and frugal, yet generous as can be to those you take to. It's a fact that you don't like everyone, and of course the same is true in reverse. It might be easier for you to understand why you can dislike than to appreciate the reverse side of the coin, for your pride can be badly dented on occasions. Scorpio brings a tendency to have down spells, though the fact that Leo is also strongly represented in your nature should prevent them from becoming a regular part of your life.

It is important for you to learn how to forgive and forget, and there isn't much point in bearing a grudge because you are basically too noble to do so. If something goes wrong, kiss the situation goodbye and get on with the next interesting adventure, of which there are many in your life. Stop–start situations sometimes get in the way, but there are plenty of people around who would be only too willing to lend a helping hand.

Scorpio with Virgo Ascendant

This is intensity carried through to the absolute. If you have a problem, it is that you fail to externalise all that is going on inside that deep, bubbling cauldron that is your inner self. Realising what you are capable of is not a problem; these only start when you have to make it plain to those around you what you want. Part of the reason for this is that you don't always understand yourself. You love intensely and would do absolutely anything for a person you are fond of, even though you might have to inconvenience yourself a great deal on the way. Relationships can cause you slight problems however, since you need to associate with people who at least come somewhere near to understanding what makes you tick. If you manage to bridge the gap between yourself and the world that constantly knocks on your door, you show yourself to be powerful, magnetic and compulsive.

There are times when you definitely prefer to stay quiet, though you do have a powerful ability to get your message across when you think it is necessary to do so. There are people around who might think that you are a push-over but they could easily get a shock when you sense that the time is right to answer back. You probably have a very orderly house and don't care for clutter of any sort.

Scorpio with Libra Ascendant

There is some tendency for you to be far more deep than the average Libran would appear to be and for this reason it is crucial that you lighten up from time to time. Every person with a Scorpio quality needs to remember that there is a happy and carefree side to all events and your Libran quality should allow you to bear this in mind. Sometimes you try to do too many things at the same time. This is fine if you take the casual overview of Libra, but less sensible when you insist on picking the last bone out of every potential, as is much more the case for Scorpio.

When worries come along, as they sometimes will, be able to listen to what your friends have to say and also realise that they are more than willing to work on your behalf, if only because you are so loyal to them. You do have a quality of self-deception, but this should not get in the way too much if you combine the instinctive actions of Libra with the deep intuition of your Scorpio component.

Probably the most important factor of this combination is your ability to succeed in a financial sense. You make a good manager, but not of the authoritarian sort. Jobs in the media or where you are expected to make up your mind quickly would suit you, because there is always an underpinning of practical sense that rarely lets you down.

THE MOON AND THE PART IT PLAYS IN YOUR LIFE

In astrology the Moon is probably the single most important heavenly body after the Sun. Its unique position, as partner to the Earth on its journey around the solar system, means that the Moon appears to pass through the signs of the zodiac extremely quickly. The zodiac position of the Moon at the time of your birth plays a great part in personal character and is especially significant in the build-up of your emotional nature.

Sun Moon Cycles

The first lunar cycle deals with the part the position of the Moon plays relative to your Sun sign. I have made the fluctuations of this pattern easy for you to understand by means of a simple cyclic graph. It appears on the first page of each 'Your Month At A Glance', under the title 'Highs and Lows'. The graph displays the lunar cycle and you will soon learn to understand how its movements have a bearing on your level of energy and your abilities.

Your Own Moon Sign

Discovering the position of the Moon at the time of your birth has always been notoriously difficult because tracking the complex zodiac positions of the Moon is not easy. This process has been reduced to three simple stages with Old Moore's unique Lunar Tables. A breakdown of the Moon's zodiac positions can be found from page 28 onwards, so that once you know what your Moon Sign is, you can see what part this plays in the overall build-up of your personal character.

If you follow the instructions on the next page you will soon be able to work out exactly what zodiac sign the Moon occupied on the day that you were born and you can then go on to compare the reading for this position with those of your Sun sign and your Ascendant. It is partly the comparison between these three important positions that goes towards making you the unique individual you are.

HOW TO DISCOVER YOUR MOON SIGN

This is a three-stage process. You may need a pen and a piece of paper but if you follow the instructions below the process should only take a minute or so.

STAGE 1 First of all you need to know the Moon Age at the time of your birth. If you look at Moon Table 1, on page 26, you will find all the years between 1917 and 2015 down the left side. Find the year of your birth and then trace across to the right to the month of your birth. Where the two intersect you will find a number. This is the date of the New Moon in the month that you were born. You now need to count forward the number of days between the New Moon and your own birthday. For example, if the New Moon in the month of your birth was shown as being the 6th and you were born on the 20th, your Moon Age Day would be 14. If the New Moon in the month of your birth came after your birthday, you need to count forward from the New Moon in the previous month. If you were born in a Leap Year, remember to count the 29th February. You can tell if your birth year was a Leap Year if the last two digits can be divided by four. Whatever the result, jot this number down so that you do not forget it.

STAGE 2 Take a look at Moon Table 2 on page 27. Down the left hand column look for the date of your birth. Now trace across to the month of your birth. Where the two meet you will find a letter. Copy this letter down alongside your Moon Age Day.

STAGE 3 Moon Table 3 on page 27 will supply you with the zodiac sign the Moon occupied on the day of your birth. Look for your Moon Age Day down the left hand column and then for the letter you found in Stage 2. Where the two converge you will find a zodiac sign and this is the sign occupied by the Moon on the day that you were born.

Your Zodiac Moon Sign Explained

You will find a profile of all zodiac Moon Signs on pages 28 to 31, showing in yet another way how astrology helps to make you into the individual that you are. In each daily entry of the Astral Diary you can find the zodiac position of the Moon for every day of the year. This also allows you to discover your lunar birthdays. Since the Moon passes through all the signs of the zodiac in about a month, you can expect something like twelve lunar birthdays each year. At these times you are likely to be emotionally steady and able to make the sort of decisions that have real, lasting value.

Moon Table I

YEAR	SEP	OCT	NOV	YEAR	SEP	OCT	NOV	YEAR	SEP	OCT	NOV
1917	15	15	14	1950	12	11	9	1983	7	6	4
1918	4	4	3	1951	1	1/30	29	1984	25	24	22
1919	23	23	22	1952	19	18	17	1985	14	14	12
1920	12	12	10	1953	8	8	6	1986	4	3	2
1921	2	1/30	29	1954	27	26	25	1987	23	22	21
1922	21	20	19	1955	16	15	14	1988	11	10	9
1923	10	10	8	1956	4	4	2	1989	29	29	28
1924	28	28	26	1957	23	23	21	1990	19	18	17
1925	18	17	16	1958	13	12	11	1991	8	8	6
1926	7	6	5	1959	3	2/31	30	1992	26	25	24
1927	25	25	24	1960	21	20	19	1993	16	15	14
1928	14	14	12	1961	10	9	8	1994	5	5	3
1929	3	2	1	1962	28	28	27	1995	24	24	22
1930	22	20	19	1963	17	17	15	1996	13	11	10
1931	12	11	9	1964	6	5	4	1997	2	2/31	30
1932	30	29	27	1965	25	24	22	1998	20	20	19
1933	19	19	17	1966	14	14	12	1999	9	9	8
1934	9	8	7	1967	4	3	2	2000	27	27	26
1935	27	27	26	1968	23	22	21	2001	17	17	16
1936	15	15	14	1969	11	10	9	2002	6	6	4
1937	4	4	3	1970	1	1/30	29	2003	26	25	24
1938	23	23	22	1971	19	19	18	2004	13	12	11
1939	13	12	11	1972	8	8	6	2005	3	2	1
1940	2	1/30	29	1973	27	26	25	2006	22	21	20
1941	21	20	19	1974	16	15	14	2007	12	11	9
1942	10	10	8	1975	5	5	3	2008	30	29	28
1943	29	29	27	1976	23	23	21	2009	19	18	17
1944	17	17	15	1977	13	12	11	2010	8	8	6
1945	6	6	4	1978	2	2/31	30	2011	27	27	25
1946	25	24	23	1979	21	20	19	2012	6	15	13
1947	14	14	12	1980	10	9	8	2013	4	4	2
1948	3	2	1	1981	28	27	26	2014	23	22	22
1949	23	21	20	1982	17	17	15	2015	13	12	11

Table 2

DAY	OCT	NOV
1	a	e
2	a	e
3	a	e
4	b	f
5	b	f
6	b	f
7	b	f
8	b	f
9	b	f
10	b	f
11	b	f
12	b	f
13	b	g
14	d	g
15	d	g
16	d	g
17	d	g
18	d	g
19	d	g
20	d	g
21	d	g
22	d	g
23	d	i
24	e	i
25	e	i
26	e	i
27	e	i
28	e	i
29	e	i
30	e	i
31	e	—

Table 3

M/D	a	b	d	e	f	g	i
0	LI	LI	LI	SC	SC	SC	SA
1	LI	LI	SC	SC	SC	SA	SA
2	LI	SC	SC	SC	SA	SA	CP
3	SC	SC	SC	SA	SA	CP	CP
4	SC	SA	SA	SA	CP	CP	CP
5	SA	SA	SA	CP	CP	AQ	AQ
6	SA	CP	CP	CP	AQ	AQ	AQ
7	SA	CP	CP	AQ	AQ	PI	PI
8	CP	CP	CP	AQ	PI	PI	PI
9	CP	AQ	AQ	AQ	PI	PI	AR
10	AQ	AQ	AQ	PI	AR	AR	AR
11	AQ	PI	PI	PI	AR	AR	TA
12	PI	PI	PI	AR	TA	TA	TA
13	PI	AR	PI	AR	TA	TA	GE
14	AR	AR	AR	TA	GE	GE	GE
15	AR	AR	AR	TA	TA	TA	GE
16	AR	AR	TA	TA	GE	GE	GE
17	AR	TA	TA	GE	GE	GE	CA
18	TA	TA	GE	GE	GE	CA	CA
19	TA	TA	GE	GE	CA	CA	CA
20	GE	GE	GE	CA	CA	CA	LE
21	GE	GE	CA	CA	CA	LE	LE
22	GE	CA	CA	CA	LE	LE	VI
23	CA	CA	CA	LE	LE	LE	VI
24	CA	CA	LE	LE	LE	VI	VI
25	CA	LE	LE	LE	VI	VI	LI
26	LE	LE	VI	VI	VI	LI	LI
27	LE	VI	VI	VI	LI	LI	SC
28	VI	VI	VI	LI	LI	LI	SC
29	VI	VI	LI	LI	LI	SC	SC

AR = Aries, TA = Taurus, GE = Gemini, CA = Cancer, LE = Leo, VI = Virgo, LI = Libra, SC = Scorpio, SA = Sagittarius, CP = Capricorn, AQ = Aquarius, PI = Pisces

MOON SIGNS

Moon in Aries

You have a strong imagination, courage, determination and a desire to do things in your own way and forge your own path through life.

Originality is a key attribute; you are seldom stuck for ideas although your mind is changeable and you could take the time to focus on individual tasks. Often quick-tempered, you take orders from few people and live life at a fast pace. Avoid health problems by taking regular time out for rest and relaxation.

Emotionally, it is important that you talk to those you are closest to and work out your true feelings. Once you discover that people are there to help, there is less necessity for you to do everything yourself.

Moon in Taurus

The Moon in Taurus gives you a courteous and friendly manner, which means you are likely to have many friends.

The good things in life mean a lot to you, as Taurus is an Earth sign that delights in experiences which please the senses. Hence you are probably a lover of good food and drink, which may in turn mean you need to keep an eye on the bathroom scales, especially as looking good is also important to you.

Emotionally you are fairly stable and you stick by your own standards. Taureans do not respond well to change. Intuition also plays an important part in your life.

Moon in Gemini

You have a warm-hearted character, sympathetic and eager to help others. At times reserved, you can also be articulate and chatty: this is part of the paradox of Gemini, which always brings duplicity to the nature. You are interested in current affairs, have a good intellect, and are good company and likely to have many friends. Most of your friends have a high opinion of you and would be ready to defend you should the need arise. However, this is usually unnecessary, as you are quite capable of defending yourself in any verbal confrontation.

Travel is important to your inquisitive mind and you find intellectual stimulus in mixing with people from different cultures. You also gain much from reading, writing and the arts but you do need plenty of rest and relaxation in order to avoid fatigue.

Moon in Cancer

The Moon in Cancer at the time of birth is a fortunate position as Cancer is the Moon's natural home. This means that the qualities of compassion and understanding given by the Moon are especially enhanced in your nature, and you are friendly and sociable and cope well with emotional pressures. You cherish home and family life, and happily do the domestic tasks. Your surroundings are important to you and you hate squalor and filth. You are likely to have a love of music and poetry.

Your basic character, although at times changeable like the Moon itself, depends on symmetry. You aim to make your surroundings comfortable and harmonious, for yourself and those close to you.

Moon in Leo

The best qualities of the Moon and Leo come together to make you warmhearted, fair, ambitious and self-confident. With good organisational abilities, you invariably rise to a position of responsibility in your chosen career. This is fortunate as you don't enjoy being an 'also-ran' and would rather be an important part of a small organisation than a menial in a large one.

You should be lucky in love, and happy, provided you put in the effort to make a comfortable home for yourself and those close to you. It is likely that you will have a love of pleasure, sport, music and literature. Life brings you many rewards, most of them as a direct result of your own efforts, although you may be luckier than average and ready to make the best of any situation.

Moon in Virgo

You are endowed with good mental abilities and a keen receptive memory, but you are never ostentatious or pretentious. Naturally quite reserved, you still have many friends, especially of the opposite sex. Marital relationships must be discussed carefully and worked at so that they remain harmonious, as personal attachments can be a problem if you do not give them your full attention.

Talented and persevering, you possess artistic qualities and are a good homemaker. Earning your honours through genuine merit, you work long and hard towards your objectives but show little pride in your achievements. Many short journeys will be undertaken in your life.

Moon in Libra

With the Moon in Libra you are naturally popular and make friends easily. People like you, probably more than you realise, you bring fun to a party and are a natural diplomat. For all its good points, Libra is not the most stable of astrological signs and, as a result, your emotions can be a little unstable too. Therefore, although the Moon in Libra is said to be good for love and marriage, your Sun sign and Rising sign will have an important effect on your emotional and loving qualities.

You must remember to relate to others in your decision-making. Co-operation is crucial because Libra represents the 'balance' of life that can only be achieved through harmonious relationships. Conformity is not easy for you because Libra, an Air sign, likes its independence.

Moon in Scorpio

Some people might call you pushy. In fact, all you really want to do is to live life to the full and protect yourself and your family from the pressures of life. Take care to avoid giving the impression of being sarcastic or impulsive and use your energies wisely and constructively.

You have great courage and you invariably achieve your goals by force of personality and sheer effort. You are fond of mystery and are good at predicting the outcome of situations and events. Travel experiences can be beneficial to you.

You may experience problems if you do not take time to examine your motives in a relationship, and also if you allow jealousy, always a feature of Scorpio, to cloud your judgement.

Moon in Sagittarius

The Moon in Sagittarius helps to make you a generous individual with humanitarian qualities and a kind heart. Restlessness may be intrinsic as your mind is seldom still. Perhaps because of this, you have a need for change that could lead you to several major moves during your adult life. You are not afraid to stand your ground when you know your judgement is right, you speak directly and have good intuition.

At work you are quick, efficient and versatile and so you make an ideal employee. You need work to be intellectually demanding and do not enjoy tedious routines.

In relationships, you anger quickly if faced with stupidity or deception, though you are just as quick to forgive and forget. Emotionally, there are times when your heart rules your head.

Moon in Capricorn

The Moon in Capricorn makes you popular and likely to come into the public eye in some way. The watery Moon is not entirely comfortable in the Earth sign of Capricorn and this may lead to some difficulties in the early years of life. An initial lack of creative ability and indecision must be overcome before the true qualities of patience and perseverance inherent in Capricorn can show through.

You have good administrative ability and are a capable worker, and if you are careful you can accumulate wealth. But you must be cautious and take professional advice in partnerships, as you are open to deception. You may be interested in social or welfare work, which suit your organisational skills and sympathy for others.

Moon in Aquarius

The Moon in Aquarius makes you an active and agreeable person with a friendly, easy-going nature. Sympathetic to the needs of others, you flourish in a laid-back atmosphere. You are broad-minded, fair and open to suggestion, although sometimes you have an unconventional quality which others can find hard to understand.

You are interested in the strange and curious, and in old articles and places. You enjoy trips to these places and gain much from them. Political, scientific and educational work interests you and you might choose a career in science or technology.

Money-wise, you make gains through innovation and concentration and Lunar Aquarians often tackle more than one job at a time. In love you are kind and honest.

Moon in Pisces

You have a kind, sympathetic nature, somewhat retiring at times, but you always take account of others' feelings and help when you can.

Personal relationships may be problematic, but as life goes on you can learn from your experiences and develop a better understanding of yourself and the world around you.

You have a fondness for travel, appreciate beauty and harmony and hate disorder and strife. You may be fond of literature and would make a good writer or speaker yourself. You have a creative imagination and may come across as an incurable romantic. You have strong intuition, maybe bordering on a mediumistic quality, which sets you apart from the mass. You may not be rich in cash terms, but your personal gifts are worth more than gold.

SCORPIO IN LOVE

Discover how compatible you are with people from the same and other parts of the zodiac. Five stars equals a match made in heaven!

Scorpio meets Scorpio

Scorpio is deep, complex and enigmatic, traits which often lead to misunderstanding with other zodiac signs, so a double Scorpio match can work well because both parties understand one another. They will allow each other periods of silence and reflection but still be willing to help, advise and support when necessary. Their relationship may seem odd to others but that doesn't matter if those involved are happy. All in all, an unusual but contented combination. Star rating: *****

Scorpio meets Sagittarius

Sagittarius needs constant stimulation and loves to be busy from dawn till dusk which may mean that it feels rather frustrated by Scorpio. Scorpions are hard workers, too, but they are also contemplative and need periods of quiet which may mean that they appear dull to Sagittarius. This could lead to a gulf between the two which must be overcome. With time and patience on both sides, this can be a lucrative encounter and good in terms of home and family. A variable alliance. Star rating: ***

Scorpio meets Capricorn

Lack of communication is the governing factor here. Neither of this pair are renowned communicators and both need a partner to draw out their full verbal potential. Consequently, Scorpio may find Capricorn cold and unapproachable while Capricorn could find Scorpio dark and brooding. Both are naturally tidy and would keep a pristine house but great effort and a mutual goal is needed on both sides to overcome the missing spark. A good match on the financial side, but probably not an earthshattering personal encounter. Star rating: **

Scorpio meets Aquarius

This is a promising and practical combination. Scorpio responds well to Aquarius' exploration of its deep nature and so this shy sign becomes lighter, brighter and more inspirational. Meanwhile, Aquarians are rarely as sure of themselves as they like to appear and are reassured by Scorpio's steady and determined support. Both signs want to be kind to the other which is a basis for a relationship that should be warm most of the time and extremely hot occasionally. Star rating: ★★★★

Scorpio meets Pisces

If ever there were two zodiac signs that have a total rapport, it has to be Scorpio and Pisces. They share very similar needs: they are not gregarious and are happy with a little silence, good music and time to contemplate the finer things in life, and both are attracted to family life. Apart, they can have a tendency to wander in a romantic sense, but this is reduced when they come together. They are deep, firm friends who enjoy each other's company and this must lead to an excellent chance of success. These people are surely made for each other! Star rating: ★★★★★

Scorpio meets Aries

There can be great affection here, even if the two signs are so very different. The common link is the planet Mars, which plays a part in both these natures. Although Aries is, outwardly, the most dominant, Scorpio people are among the most powerful to be found anywhere. This quiet determination is respected by Aries. Aries will satisfy the passionate side of Scorpio, particularly with instruction from Scorpio. There are mysteries here which will add spice to life. The few arguments that do occur are likely to be awe-inspiring. Star rating: ★★★★

Scorpio meets Taurus

Scorpio is deep – very deep – which may be a problem, because Taurus doesn't wear its heart on its sleeve either. It might be difficult for this pair to get together, because neither is naturally inclined to make the first move. Taurus stands in awe of the power and intensity of the Scorpio mind, while the Scorpion is interested in the Bull's affable and friendly qualities, so an enduring relationship could be forged if the couple ever get round to talking. Both are lovers of home and family, which will help to cement a relationship. Star rating: **

Scorpio meets Gemini

There could be problems here. Scorpio is one of the deepest and least understood of all the zodiac signs, which at first seems like a challenge to intellectual Gemini, who thinks it can solve anything. But the deeper the Gemini digs, the further down Scorpio goes. Meanwhile, Scorpio may be finding Gemini thoughtless, shallow and even downright annoying. Gemini is often afraid of Scorpio's perception and strength, together with the sting in the Scorpion's tail. Anything is possible, but the outlook for this match is less than promising. Star rating: **

Scorpio meets Cancer

This match is potentially a great success, a fact which is often a mystery to astrologers. Some feel it is due to the compatibility of the Water element, but it could also come from a mixture of similarity and difference in the personalities. Scorpio is partly ruled by Mars, which gives it a deep, passionate, dominant and powerful side. Cancerians generally like and respect this amalgam, and recognise something there that they would like to adopt themselves. On the other side of the coin, Scorpio needs love and emotional security which Cancer offers generously. Star rating: *****

Scorpio meets Leo

Stand back and watch the sparks fly! Scorpio has the deep sensitivity of a Water sign but it is also partially ruled by Fire planet Mars, from which it draws great power, and Leo will find that difficult. Leo loves to take charge and really hates to feel psychologically undermined, which is Scorpio's stock-in-trade. Scorpio may find Leo's ideals a little shallow, which will be upsetting to the Lion. Anything is possible, but this possibility is rather slimmer than most. Star rating: **

Scorpio meets Virgo

There are one or two potential difficulties here, but there is also a meeting point from which to overcome them. Virgo is very caring and protective, a trait which Scorpio understands and even emulates. Scorpio will impress Virgo with its serious side. Both signs are consistent, although also sarcastic. Scorpio may uncover a hidden passion in Virgo which all too often lies deep within its Earth-sign nature. Material success is very likely, with Virgo taking the lion's share of the domestic chores and family responsibilities. Star rating: ***

Scorpio meets Libra

Many astrologers have reservations about this match because, on the surface, the signs are so different. However, this couple may find fulfilment because these differences mean that their respective needs are met. Scorpio needs a partner to lighten the load, which won't daunt Libra, while Libra looks for a steadfast quality which it doesn't possess, but which Scorpio can supply naturally. Financial success is possible because they both have good ideas and back them up with hard work and determination. All in all, a promising outlook. Star rating: ****

VENUS:
THE PLANET OF LOVE

If you look up at the sky around sunset or sunrise you will often see Venus in close attendance to the Sun. It is arguably one of the most beautiful sights of all and there is little wonder that historically it became associated with the goddess of love. But although Venus does play an important part in the way you view love and in the way others see you romantically, this is only one of the spheres of influence that it enjoys in your overall character.

Venus has a part to play in the more cultured side of your life and has much to do with your appreciation of art, literature, music and general creativity. Even the way you look is responsive to the part of the zodiac that Venus occupied at the start of your life, though this fact is also down to your Sun sign and Ascending sign. If, at the time you were born, Venus occupied one of the more gregarious zodiac signs, you will be more likely to wear your heart on your sleeve, as well as to be more attracted to entertainment, social gatherings and good company. If on the other hand Venus occupied a quiet zodiac sign at the time of your birth, you would tend to be more retiring and less willing to shine in public situations.

It's good to know what part the planet Venus plays in your life, for it can have a great bearing on the way you appear to the rest of the world and since we all have to mix with others, you can learn to make the very best of what Venus has to offer you.

One of the great complications in the past has always been trying to establish exactly what zodiac position Venus enjoyed when you were born, because the planet is notoriously difficult to track. However, I have solved that problem by creating a table that is exclusive to your Sun sign, which you will find on the following page.

Establishing your Venus sign could not be easier. Just look up the year of your birth on the page opposite and you will see a sign of the zodiac. This was the sign that Venus occupied in the period covered by your sign in that year. If Venus occupied more than one sign during the period, this is indicated by the date on which the sign changed, and the name of the new sign. For instance, if you were born in 1950, Venus was in Libra until the 28th October, after which time it was in Scorpio. If you were born before 28th October your Venus sign is Libra, if you were born on or after 28th October, your Venus sign is Scorpio. Once you have established the position of Venus at the time of your birth, you can then look in the pages which follow to see how this has a bearing on your life as a whole.

1916 VIRGO / 3.11 LIBRA
1917 SAGITTARIUS / 7.11 CAPRICORN
1918 LIBRA / 30.10 SCORPIO
1919 VIRGO / 9.11 LIBRA
1920 SCORPIO / 24.10 SAGITTARIUS/
    17.11 CAPRICORN
1921 LIBRA / 14.11 SCORPIO
1922 SAGITTARIUS / 16.11 SCORPIO
1923 SCORPIO / 9.11 SAGITTARIUS
1924 VIRGO / 3.11 LIBRA
1925 SAGITTARIUS / 7.11 CAPRICORN
1926 LIBRA / 29.10 SCORPIO
1927 VIRGO / 10.11 LIBRA
1928 SAGITTARIUS /
    17.11 CAPRICORN
1929 LIBRA / 13.11 SCORPIO
1930 SAGITTARIUS / 16.11 SCORPIO
1931 SCORPIO / 8.11 SAGITTARIUS
1932 VIRGO / 2.11 LIBRA
1933 SAGITTARIUS / 7.11 CAPRICORN
1934 LIBRA / 29.10 SCORPIO
1935 VIRGO / 10.11 LIBRA
1936 SAGITTARIUS /
    16.11 CAPRICORN
1937 LIBRA / 13.11 SCORPIO
1938 SAGITTARIUS / 16.11 SCORPIO
1939 SCORPIO / 7.11 SAGITTARIUS
1940 VIRGO / 2.11 LIBRA
1941 SAGITTARIUS / 7.11 CAPRICORN
1942 LIBRA / 28.10 SCORPIO
1943 VIRGO / 10.11 LIBRA
1944 SAGITTARIUS /
    16.11 CAPRICORN
1945 LIBRA / 13.11 SCORPIO
1946 SAGITTARIUS / 16.11 SCORPIO
1947 SCORPIO / 6.11 SAGITTARIUS
1948 VIRGO / 1.11 LIBRA
1949 SAGITTARIUS / 6.11 CAPRICORN
1950 LIBRA / 28.10 SCORPIO
1951 VIRGO / 10.11 LIBRA
1952 SAGITTARIUS /
    16.11 CAPRICORN
1953 LIBRA / 12.11 SCORPIO
1954 SAGITTARIUS / 28.10 SCORPIO
1955 SCORPIO / 6.11 SAGITTARIUS
1956 VIRGO / 1.11 LIBRA
1957 SAGITTARIUS / 6.11 CAPRICORN
1958 LIBRA / 27.10 SCORPIO
1959 VIRGO / 10.11 LIBRA
1960 SAGITTARIUS /
    15.11 CAPRICORN
1961 LIBRA / 12.11 SCORPIO
1962 SAGITTARIUS / 28.10 SCORPIO
1963 SCORPIO / 5.11 SAGITTARIUS
1964 VIRGO / 31.10 LIBRA
1965 SAGITTARIUS / 6.11 CAPRICORN

1966 LIBRA / 27.10 SCORPIO
1967 VIRGO / 10.11 LIBRA
1968 SAGITTARIUS /
    15.11 CAPRICORN
1969 LIBRA / 11.11 SCORPIO
1970 SAGITTARIUS / 28.10 SCORPIO
1971 SCORPIO / 4.11 SAGITTARIUS
1972 VIRGO / 31.10 LIBRA
1973 SAGITTARIUS / 6.11 CAPRICORN
1974 LIBRA / 26.10 SCORPIO
1975 VIRGO / 9.11 LIBRA
1976 SAGITTARIUS /
    15.11 CAPRICORN
1977 LIBRA / 11.11 SCORPIO
1978 SAGITTARIUS / 28.10 SCORPIO
1979 SCORPIO / 4.11 SAGITTARIUS
1980 VIRGO / 30.10 LIBRA
1981 SAGITTARIUS / 5.11 CAPRICORN
1982 LIBRA / 26.10 SCORPIO
1983 VIRGO / 9.11 LIBRA
1984 SAGITTARIUS /
    14.11 CAPRICORN
1985 LIBRA / 10.11 SCORPIO
1986 SAGITTARIUS / 28.10 SCORPIO
1987 SCORPIO / 3.11 SAGITTARIUS
1988 VIRGO / 30.10 LIBRA
1989 SAGITTARIUS / 5.11 CAPRICORN
1990 LIBRA / 25.10 SCORPIO
1991 VIRGO / 9.11 LIBRA
1992 SAGITTARIUS /
    14.11 CAPRICORN
1993 LIBRA / 10.11 SCORPIO
1994 SAGITTARIUS / 28.10 SCORPIO
1995 SCORPIO / 3.11 SAGITTARIUS
1996 VIRGO / 29.10 LIBRA
1997 SAGITTARIUS / 5.11 CAPRICORN
1998 LIBRA / 25.10 SCORPIO
1999 VIRGO / 9.11 LIBRA
2000 SAGITTARIUS /
    14.11 CAPRICORN
2001 LIBRA / 10.11 SCORPIO
2002 SAGITTARIUS / 28.10 SCORPIO
2003 SCORPIO / 3.11 SAGITTARIUS
2004 VIRGO / 29.10 LIBRA
2005 SAGITTARIUS / 5.11 CAPRICORN
2006 LIBRA / 25.10 SCORPIO
2007 VIRGO / 9.11 LIBRA
2008 SAGITTARIUS / 14.11
    CAPRICORN
2009 LIBRA / 10.11 SCORPIO
2010 SAGITTARIUS / 28.10 SCORPIO
2011 SCORPIO / 3.11 SAGITTARIUS
2012 VIRGO / 29.10 LIBRA
2013 SAGITTARIUS / 5.11 CAPRICORN
2014 LIBRA / 25.10 SCORPIO
2015 VIRGO / 9.11 LIBRA

VENUS THROUGH THE ZODIAC SIGNS

Venus in Aries

Amongst other things, the position of Venus in Aries indicates a fondness for travel, music and all creative pursuits. Your nature tends to be affectionate and you would try not to create confusion or difficulty for others if it could be avoided. Many people with this planetary position have a great love of the theatre, and mental stimulation is of the greatest importance. Early romantic attachments are common with Venus in Aries, so it is very important to establish a genuine sense of romantic continuity. Early marriage is not recommended, especially if it is based on sympathy. You may give your heart a little too readily on occasions.

Venus in Taurus

You are capable of very deep feelings and your emotions tend to last for a very long time. This makes you a trusting partner and lover, whose constancy is second to none. In life you are precise and careful and always try to do things the right way. Although this means an ordered life, which you are comfortable with, it can also lead you to be rather too fussy for your own good. Despite your pleasant nature, you are very fixed in your opinions and quite able to speak your mind. Others are attracted to you and historical astrologers always quoted this position of Venus as being very fortunate in terms of marriage. However, if you find yourself involved in a failed relationship, it could take you a long time to trust again.

Venus in Gemini

As with all associations related to Gemini, you tend to be quite versatile, anxious for change and intelligent in your dealings with the world at large. You may gain money from more than one source but you are equally good at spending it. There is an inference here that you are a good communicator, via either the written or the spoken word, and you love to be in the company of interesting people. Always on the look-out for culture, you may also be very fond of music, and love to indulge the curious and cultured side of your nature. In romance you tend to have more than one relationship and could find yourself associated with someone who has previously been a friend or even a distant relative.

Venus in Cancer

You often stay close to home because you are very fond of family and enjoy many of your most treasured moments when you are with those you love. Being naturally sympathetic, you will always do anything you can to support those around you, even people you hardly know at all. This charitable side of your nature is your most noticeable trait and is one of the reasons why others are naturally so fond of you. Being receptive and in some cases even psychic, you can see through to the soul of most of those with whom you come into contact. You may not commence too many romantic attachments but when you do give your heart, it tends to be unconditionally.

Venus in Leo

It must become quickly obvious to almost anyone you meet that you are kind, sympathetic and yet determined enough to stand up for anyone or anything that is truly important to you. Bright and sunny, you warm the world with your natural enthusiasm and would rarely do anything to hurt those around you, or at least not intentionally. In romance you are ardent and sincere, though some may find your style just a little overpowering. Gains come through your contacts with other people and this could be especially true with regard to romance, for love and money often come hand in hand for those who were born with Venus in Leo. People claim to understand you, though you are more complex than you seem.

Venus in Virgo

Your nature could well be fairly quiet no matter what your Sun sign might be, though this fact often manifests itself as an inner peace and would not prevent you from being basically sociable. Some delays and even the odd disappointment in love cannot be ruled out with this planetary position, though it's a fact that you will usually find the happiness you look for in the end. Catapulting yourself into romantic entanglements that you know to be rather ill-advised is not sensible, and it would be better to wait before you committed yourself exclusively to any one person. It is the essence of your nature to serve the world at large and through doing so it is possible that you will attract money at some stage in your life.

Venus in Libra

Venus is very comfortable in Libra and bestows upon those people who have this planetary position a particular sort of kindness that is easy to recognise. This is a very good position for all sorts of friendships and also for romantic attachments that usually bring much joy into your life. Few individuals with Venus in Libra would avoid marriage and since you are capable of great depths of love, it is likely that you will find a contented personal life. You like to mix with people of integrity and intelligence but don't take kindly to scruffy surroundings or work that means getting your hands too dirty. Careful speculation, good business dealings and money through marriage all seem fairly likely.

Venus in Scorpio

You are quite open and tend to spend money quite freely, even on those occasions when you don't have very much. Although your intentions are always good, there are times when you get yourself in to the odd scrape and this can be particularly true when it comes to romance, which you may come to late or from a rather unexpected direction. Certainly you have the power to be happy and to make others contented on the way, but you find the odd stumbling block on your journey through life and it could seem that you have to work harder than those around you. As a result of this, you gain a much deeper understanding of the true value of personal happiness than many people ever do, and are likely to achieve true contentment in the end.

Venus in Sagittarius

You are lighthearted, cheerful and always able to see the funny side of any situation. These facts enhance your popularity, which is especially high with members of the opposite sex. You should never have to look too far to find romantic interest in your life, though it is just possible that you might be too willing to commit yourself before you are certain that the person in question is right for you. Part of the problem here extends to other areas of life too. The fact is that you like variety in everything and so can tire of situations that fail to offer it. All the same, if you choose wisely and learn to understand your restless side, then great happiness can be yours.

Venus in Capricorn

The most notable trait that comes from Venus in this position is that it makes you trustworthy and able to take on all sorts of responsibilities in life. People are instinctively fond of you and love you all the more because you are always ready to help those who are in any form of need. Social and business popularity can be yours and there is a magnetic quality to your nature that is particularly attractive in a romantic sense. Anyone who wants a partner for a lover, a spouse and a good friend too would almost certainly look in your direction. Constancy is the hallmark of your nature and unfaithfulness would go right against the grain. You might sometimes be a little too trusting.

Venus in Aquarius

This location of Venus offers a fondness for travel and a desire to try out something new at every possible opportunity. You are extremely easy to get along with and tend to have many friends from varied backgrounds, classes and inclinations. You like to live a distinct sort of life and gain a great deal from moving about, both in a career sense and with regard to your home. It is not out of the question that you could form a romantic attachment to someone who comes from far away or be attracted to a person of a distinctly artistic and original nature. What you cannot stand is jealousy, for you have friends of both sexes and would want to keep things that way.

Venus in Pisces

The first thing people tend to notice about you is your wonderful, warm smile. Being very charitable by nature you will do anything to help others, even if you don't know them well. Much of your life may be spent sorting out situations for other people, but it is very important to feel that you are living for yourself too. In the main, you remain cheerful, and tend to be quite attractive to members of the opposite sex. Where romantic attachments are concerned, you could be drawn to people who are significantly older or younger than yourself or to someone with a unique career or point of view. It might be best for you to avoid marrying whilst you are still very young.

HOW THE DIAGRAMS WORK

Through the picture diagrams in the Astral Diary I want to help you to plot your year. With them you can see where the positive and negative aspects will be found in each month. To make the most of them, all you have to do is remember where and when!

Let me show you how they work ...

THE MONTH AT A GLANCE

Just as there are twelve separate zodiac signs, so astrologers believe that each sign has twelve separate aspects to life. Each of the twelve segments relates to a different personal aspect. I list them all every month so that their meanings are always clear.

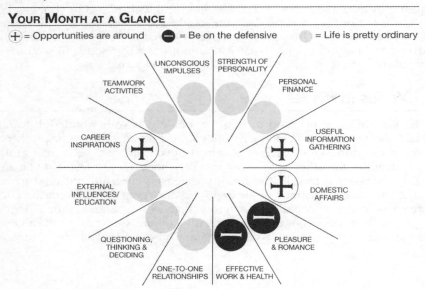

YOUR MONTH AT A GLANCE

+ = Opportunities are around   − = Be on the defensive   = Life is pretty ordinary

UNCONSCIOUS IMPULSES
STRENGTH OF PERSONALITY
TEAMWORK ACTIVITIES
PERSONAL FINANCE
CAREER INSPIRATIONS
USEFUL INFORMATION GATHERING
EXTERNAL INFLUENCES/ EDUCATION
DOMESTIC AFFAIRS
QUESTIONING, THINKING & DECIDING
PLEASURE & ROMANCE
ONE-TO-ONE RELATIONSHIPS
EFFECTIVE WORK & HEALTH

I have designed this chart to show you how and when these twelve different aspects are being influenced throughout the year. When there is a shaded circle, nothing out of the ordinary is to be expected. However, when a circle turns white with a plus sign, the influence is positive. Where the circle is black with a minus sign, it is a negative.

YOUR ENERGY RHYTHM CHART

Below is a picture diagram in which I link your zodiac group to the rhythm of the Moon. In doing this I have calculated when you will be gaining strength from its influence and equally when you may be weakened by it.

If you think of yourself as being like the tides of the ocean then you may understand how your own energies must also rise and fall. And if you understand how it works and when it is working, then you can better organise your activities to achieve more and get things done more easily.

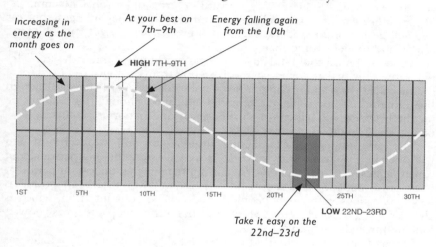

THE KEY DAYS

Some of the entries are in **bold**, which indicates the working of astrological cycles in your life. Look out for them each week as they are the best days to take action or make decisions. The daily text tells you which area of your life to focus on.

MERCURY RETROGRADE

The Mercury symbol (☿) indicates that Mercury is retrograde on that day. Since Mercury governs communication, the fact that it appears to be moving backwards when viewed from the Earth at this time should warn you that your communication skills are not likely to be at their best and you could expect some setbacks.

SCORPIO: YOUR YEAR IN BRIEF

The year might start quite slowly, but you can at least be sure that it will also be steady and that you will begin to make progress almost immediately. January and February allow you to consolidate gains you made late last year and you will also be moving forward in terms of personal attachments. Money is likely to be better in February but even at the beginning of the year you will be full of good ideas. This is definitely a time to get your thinking cap on and to make some changes.

March and April could still be somewhat quiet at times, but with interludes of intense activity that seem to come like a bolt from the blue. You need to be on the ball at work and making professional strides on a daily basis. Although there might be some reorganisation and upheaval at home, this tends to be for the best and you will also be making new and important contacts. New people can bring revolutionary ideas.

The early summer, May and June, should allow you to travel more and will offer new opportunities at work, as well as strengthening personal and romantic ties. You may feel that you are approaching an important period at work or in some practical sense and you certainly won't have any problems in your dealings with other people. This is when your intuition, which is always strong, begins to grow. Seeing through other people is as easy now as looking through a window.

July and August are the hot months and should certainly be sizzling as far as you are concerned. Scorpio is really on form now and likely to take any opportunity to shine, especially in a romantic sense. With everything to play for, this is a time to make everyone envious of your wonderful nature. Easy-going but attentive, you are able to work and play equally effectively. Some Scorpio people may now be thinking in terms of a change of occupation.

September and October may be slightly quieter, but not much. You are likely to turn your focus in the direction of your work and concentrate on making progress. Alterations to your working routines and a need to take on new responsibilities are symptomatic of this period. Love shines brightly through the autumn for many Scorpio subjects and if you are in a settled relationship you can pep things up.

The last two months of the year, November and December, should find you on top form and anxious to enjoy anything that is happening around you. You are making most of the running and you show the world just how positive and aspirational you are. Look out for significant gains, both in terms of money and responsibility, and do your best to make Christmas extra special for everyone around you.

January
2015

Your Month at a Glance

(+) = Opportunities are around   (−) = Be on the defensive   ◯ = Life is pretty ordinary

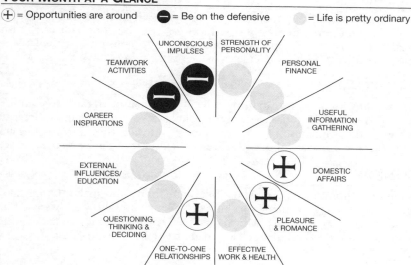

- UNCONSCIOUS IMPULSES
- STRENGTH OF PERSONALITY
- TEAMWORK ACTIVITIES
- PERSONAL FINANCE
- CAREER INSPIRATIONS
- USEFUL INFORMATION GATHERING
- EXTERNAL INFLUENCES/ EDUCATION
- DOMESTIC AFFAIRS
- QUESTIONING, THINKING & DECIDING
- PLEASURE & ROMANCE
- ONE-TO-ONE RELATIONSHIPS
- EFFECTIVE WORK & HEALTH

January Highs and Lows

Here I show you how the rhythms of the Moon will affect you this month. Like the tide, your energies and abilities will rise and fall with its pattern. When it is above the centre line, go for it, when it is below, you should be resting.

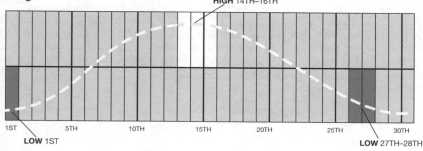

HIGH 14TH–16TH

LOW 1ST

LOW 27TH–28TH

45

I THURSDAY
Moon Age Day 11 Moon Sign Taurus

Family responsibilities will probably have to take second place in your thinking now, as the real practical necessities of life get underway after a prolonged Christmas break. Many Scorpio subjects will now be straining at the leash and just aching to get things moving, but your interests are best served by being patient.

2 FRIDAY
Moon Age Day 12 Moon Sign Gemini

Now you are more likely than ever to find yourself in the social limelight: possibly not the most interesting position for you, but one you can relish nevertheless. There are some new arrangements to consider, particularly at home, as relatives suddenly decide they don't like things the way they are.

3 SATURDAY
Moon Age Day 13 Moon Sign Gemini

Your present winning ways can bring a distinctly romantic streak into your life around this time. The lunar low is well gone and you have plenty of energy and a fixed determination regarding the way you want things to be. Others pick up on this, especially those who are very close to you in a personal sense.

4 SUNDAY
Moon Age Day 14 Moon Sign Gemini

Expand your horizons at every possible opportunity and make the most of what can be a really excellent sort of week. Your know-how shows itself at every turn, emphasising the practical qualities that are so much a part of your personality. Rules and regulations are made to be bent or broken today.

5 MONDAY
Moon Age Day 15 Moon Sign Cancer

There are signs that this could be a very busy time at work and a period during which you have little or no time to cast your mind homeward. This can be rather unnerving for your zodiac sign, because a part of you never leaves the comfort and security of your abode. You need to be as positive as possible.

6 TUESDAY
Moon Age Day 16 Moon Sign Cancer

Popularity remains generally high and you can take advantage of this fact. Those around you seem eminently reasonable and quite willing to take your ideas on board. Get as much done as early in the day as proves to be possible, leaving yourself with some personal time later on.

7 WEDNESDAY
Moon Age Day 17 Moon Sign Leo

Such is the competitive edge and the fund of ideas that is flowing through you today that you want to be the first at work. Be careful, though, there is just a chance you will exhaust yourself and that won't really be much help in the longer term. What works best today is 'slow and steady wins the race'.

8 THURSDAY
Moon Age Day 18 Moon Sign Leo

This might prove to be a period of some instability, which means you reacting to situations rather than creating them. Although this can be quite uncomfortable, you are probably going to be better off because of it. Originality is what this period is all about and if it comes from elsewhere, who cares?

9 FRIDAY
Moon Age Day 19 Moon Sign Virgo

Good times are on the way in your social life, even if you are having slightly more difficulties where work is concerned. Best of all is romance, because it is in this sphere of your life that you achieve the greatest degree of happiness right now. In business matters, you could prove rather too blunt for your own good.

10 SATURDAY
Moon Age Day 20 Moon Sign Virgo

Personal encounters can be particularly surprising at this time, but perhaps not all that odd when you realise what a very peculiar day this can also turn out to be in other ways. The unusual becomes commonplace and you will need to use every bit of your intuition in order to work out the reason for almost any event.

11 SUNDAY
Moon Age Day 21 Moon Sign Virgo

Your desire to get together with others this weekend is strong and you will probably put aside some of the usual considerations in order to socialise. You might enjoy an outing of some sort and can even do practical things, just as long as there is someone else around with whom you can have a good chat.

12 MONDAY
Moon Age Day 22 Moon Sign Libra

You can succeed particularly well in partnerships at the beginning of this working week and might find that you are getting on especially well with people who meant little to you in the past. Because you are able to modify your own nature, all sorts of new avenues are now open to you.

13 TUESDAY
Moon Age Day 23 Moon Sign Libra

Meeting people, travelling, reading and writing are all possibilities under present trends. The more you learn about life, the more fascinated you become. This is likely to be a very varied day during which you are fully committed to meshing with the world around you.

14 WEDNESDAY
Moon Age Day 24 Moon Sign Scorpio

Now is a period for putting new initiatives to the test and for getting on extremely well in life generally. In a social sense, it is clear that you are sparkling like the morning sun, which offers all sorts of possibilities. You can afford to push your luck a little and should expect to make gains.

15 THURSDAY
Moon Age Day 25 Moon Sign Scorpio

There is great room for using your intuition and your practical skills this Thursday. Although someone is more or less bound to feel left out, it is imperative that you follow your own mind, no matter where it takes you. The slower types will simply have to catch up when they can.

16 FRIDAY
Moon Age Day 26 Moon Sign Scorpio

Certain issues at work might seem to be more trouble than they are worth now. That means leaving them alone and certainly does not indicate a period during which you should blow them up out of all proportion. With plenty to play for in the relationship stakes, don't be too embarrassed to tell people how you feel.

17 SATURDAY
Moon Age Day 27 Moon Sign Sagittarius

You can really impress others, and at most levels of your life. Attitudes vary in your friendship circle and it will become clear that you cannot back everyone's point of view. Neither can you rely on diplomacy. The time has come to answer truthfully any question you are asked.

18 SUNDAY
Moon Age Day 28 Moon Sign Sagittarius

The message today is to get busy and to stay that way for most of the day. If it isn't possible, you should at least make some attempt to look as though you are doing something important. This is especially true if you are at work, where superiors are taking a great interest in your capacity to get things done.

19 MONDAY

Moon Age Day 29 Moon Sign Capricorn

There are practical situations around at the moment and you will want to take full advantage of them. You can get things done at home and seem to have a particularly good ability to organise and arrange things. All in all, this will turn out to be a busy day during which you find yourself working to your full potential.

20 TUESDAY

Moon Age Day 0 Moon Sign Capricorn

Compromises are difficult to make today, especially with people at work. The fact is that you know what you want and if those around you get in the way, the responsibility is likely to be theirs. Scorpio can be quite vindictive and even a little destructive on occasions. Make sure you are not that way now.

21 WEDNESDAY

Moon Age Day 1 Moon Sign Aquarius

You are out and about and busy doing things that please you, but that doesn't leave much time for stopping and looking. Activity is what counts and it seems as though good fortune favours your efforts once again. Arguments are likely to arise at home, but they won't help your case at all, so keep out of them.

22 THURSDAY ☿

Moon Age Day 2 Moon Sign Aquarius

There are signs that this could be a good day at work. If you are without an occupation now, but looking for one, this is as good a time as any to concentrate your efforts. On a more personal level, you could discover that you have an admirer now that you would never have suspected.

23 FRIDAY ☿

Moon Age Day 3 Moon Sign Pisces

Changing your mind at the last minute is something you are apt to do today and tomorrow. This may not be a wise strategy. It would probably be better to think ahead and to stick to your decisions. The last thing you need to be accused of at the moment is jumping from foot to foot.

24 SATURDAY ☿

Moon Age Day 4 Moon Sign Pisces

This ought to be a happy phase at home, though with less going for it at work. You tend to stick to what you know at present and won't be all that comfortable when facing situations you don't understand all that well or are confused by. Comfort and security seem to mean a great deal to you this weekend.

25 SUNDAY ☿ *Moon Age Day 5 Moon Sign Aries*

At the moment, making progress means being in the know. That is why you have to keep your eyes and ears open. The more you pay attention to what is happening around you, the greater your chance of keeping up. This is particularly true for working Scorpio people who hold significant responsibility.

26 MONDAY ☿ *Moon Age Day 6 Moon Sign Aries*

The current pace of activity shows no signs at all of slowing. Remember that you are only human and, if necessary, force yourself into a way of living that allows time for rest and reflection. It might be possible to look at your routines and itemise those jobs that could easily wait until later.

27 TUESDAY ☿ *Moon Age Day 7 Moon Sign Taurus*

Things are quieter today and tomorrow and there appears to be very little you can do about the situation. You can thank the lunar low for the present state of affairs and should simply jog along as best you can. There may be some light relief coming from the comical behaviour of family members.

28 WEDNESDAY ☿ *Moon Age Day 8 Moon Sign Taurus*

As long as you keep your hopes and dreams realistic, there is really no reason why today should work against you. Of course, it could be slow going, but that is hardly likely to bother you all that much. What matters is the big picture and that looks as bright and hopeful as ever.

29 THURSDAY ☿ *Moon Age Day 9 Moon Sign Gemini*

Career and material plans appear to be on the up, but you may be restrained, as if by some giant invisible elastic band. No matter how hard you try to push forward, something pulls you back. Don't worry; this is a state of affairs that won't last beyond today. On the positive side, this can be a very funny interlude.

30 FRIDAY ☿ *Moon Age Day 10 Moon Sign Gemini*

There is a slight possibility of strong disagreements cropping up today. Such a state of affairs will only happen if those around you insist on being right all the time. For your own part, the position of Mars in your chart now can make you stubborn and unwilling to admit that you could just be wrong about something.

31 SATURDAY ☿

Moon Age Day 11   Moon Sign Gemini

What you hear from others today can easily contribute to your fund of knowledge, so don't hold back when it comes to listening in. If you are accused of being nosy, you will simply have to shrug your shoulders because basically it's true at the moment. However, the rewards for paying attention can be great.

February 2015

YOUR MONTH AT A GLANCE

(+) = Opportunities are around   (—) = Be on the defensive   = Life is pretty ordinary

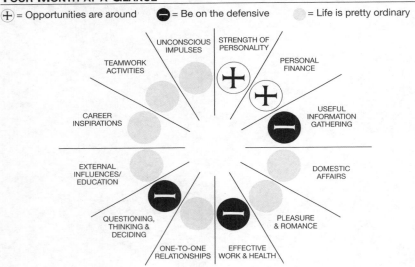

UNCONSCIOUS IMPULSES
STRENGTH OF PERSONALITY
TEAMWORK ACTIVITIES
PERSONAL FINANCE
CAREER INSPIRATIONS
USEFUL INFORMATION GATHERING
EXTERNAL INFLUENCES/ EDUCATION
DOMESTIC AFFAIRS
QUESTIONING, THINKING & DECIDING
PLEASURE & ROMANCE
ONE-TO-ONE RELATIONSHIPS
EFFECTIVE WORK & HEALTH

FEBRUARY HIGHS AND LOWS

Here I show you how the rhythms of the Moon will affect you this month. Like the tide, your energies and abilities will rise and fall with its pattern. When it is above the centre line, go for it, when it is below, you should be resting.

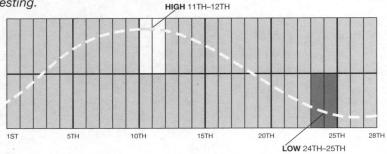

HIGH 11TH–12TH

1ST   5TH   10TH   15TH   20TH   25TH   28TH

LOW 24TH–25TH

1 SUNDAY ☿ *Moon Age Day 12 Moon Sign Cancer*

Only you can decide whether you want to continue in a direction you have previously chosen or to change your mind. There is nothing at all wrong with modifying your opinions, even if you have to explain your decision to someone else. There could be some small financial gains around this time.

2 MONDAY ☿ *Moon Age Day 13 Moon Sign Cancer*

Fulfil your need for variety and stimulation in just about any way you can today. If it is possible to take the day off work then so much the better. You are good company and great to be around generally. If there any frustrations at all today, these come from the direction of people who simply won't adapt.

3 TUESDAY ☿ *Moon Age Day 14 Moon Sign Leo*

You are involved in a period of major changes, some of which you haven't even chosen yourself. Having constantly to adapt isn't necessarily easy for your zodiac sign, but it is very important. If you can manage to shrug your shoulders and simply watch what is happening around you, so much the better.

4 WEDNESDAY ☿ *Moon Age Day 15 Moon Sign Leo*

Apart from good trends in personal finances, this may be a rewarding time for renewing aspects of your personal life. You won't be making too many mistakes either at work or at home and you should find yourself surrounded by people who quite obviously like you.

5 THURSDAY ☿ *Moon Age Day 16 Moon Sign Leo*

Your talent for understanding others has rarely been better than it is at the moment, so this would be a good time to sort out the problems of a friend or even a family member. When it comes to advice you are seeking rather than offering, you should turn to a wise old pal.

6 FRIDAY ☿ *Moon Age Day 17 Moon Sign Virgo*

Scorpios are natural seekers of wisdom, a search that can lead to many journeys and a good deal of study. In this frame of mind you are led to a state of intellectual curiosity. There is much that is unusual about this part of February but it does make sense to you in a peculiar sort of way.

7 SATURDAY ☿ *Moon Age Day 18 Moon Sign Virgo*

Any form of philosophical interest continues to appeal to you now, especially if it is allied to physical exercise. This is the reason that so many Scorpio subjects interest themselves in subjects such as yoga. Workouts for their own sake are not so interesting and so a search for the right path might be beginning.

8 SUNDAY ☿ *Moon Age Day 19 Moon Sign Libra*

You enjoy the stimulation that can come from travel now, and the fact that the year is so new and winter is probably at its worst has little to do with the situation. You need a change of scenery and it doesn't really matter where you choose to go. If you avoid this issue, you might well end up down in the dumps.

9 MONDAY ☿ *Moon Age Day 20 Moon Sign Libra*

Learning experiences remain pleasurable and offer you the chance to see yourself in a very different light. It might occur to you around now that much of what has been happening recently has had a very selfish aspect to it. This could be true but even your caring zodiac sign is allowed to be selfish sometimes.

10 TUESDAY ☿ *Moon Age Day 21 Moon Sign Libra*

Personal relationships may be somewhat more troublesome than has been the case of late. Your partner could prove to be emotionally demanding and you won't have all the answers to the problems that family members are posing. Part of the reason for this is the present position of the Moon.

11 WEDNESDAY ☿ *Moon Age Day 22 Moon Sign Scorpio*

With less desire to upturn the apple cart of life, you are now simply keen to enjoy yourself and to help those around you do the same. You can expect a good deal from personal attachments, and if you don't have a partner at the moment there are likely to be offers in store. Lady Luck is on your side.

12 THURSDAY ☿ *Moon Age Day 23 Moon Sign Scorpio*

Many of your thoughts are fleeting now, but the mental activity that creates them is endless. You are at your happiest today when your versatility is finding useful outlets. New and positive beginnings are possible, not least in terms of friendships – or maybe the complete rebuilding of existing ones.

13 FRIDAY ☿
Moon Age Day 24 Moon Sign Sagittarius

The desire for personal transformation continues, probably to a greater extent than has been the case for a number of months. Once the sign of Scorpio gets itself into this frame of mind, just about everyone get to know about it! Although you are very keen to make alterations, do so by consensus and not argument.

14 SATURDAY
Moon Age Day 25 Moon Sign Sagittarius

You can look forward to a good deal of optimism today from yourself and those around you. Take a holiday from all the reorganisation and do something that purely and simply appeals to you. It doesn't have to be important or financially rewarding. All that matters is that you have a good time.

15 SUNDAY
Moon Age Day 26 Moon Sign Capricorn

The desire for freedom is strong now, though this doesn't necessarily mean you intend to fly off to some exotic location. The sort of freedom you seek has much more to do with being able to go about your life in the way you would wish. If others impede those rights, it's time to tell them.

16 MONDAY
Moon Age Day 27 Moon Sign Capricorn

Today should be quite favourable for adventure or any sort of travel. Although there are slight setbacks to be dealt with from time to time, in the main you find that you can make significant progress. Don't be too quick to take the word of a stranger over that of a friend, even if you are at first convinced.

17 TUESDAY
Moon Age Day 28 Moon Sign Aquarius

You seem to be the life and soul of any party that is taking place around you right now, even if some of them are arranged at very short notice. Give yourself a pat on the back for a recent job well done, but don't stand still. It's time to move on in one way or another, so keep up the effort.

18 WEDNESDAY
Moon Age Day 29 Moon Sign Aquarius

Social activities take centre stage today, partly because it will be difficult to get ahead in other ways. Practical jobs are likely to remain undone and you will need to show a good deal of patience when dealing with wayward family members. This is a day to keep busy.

19 THURSDAY
Moon Age Day 0 Moon Sign Pisces

Objectives that are now on the drawing board need looking at very carefully before you commit yourself in any way. Confidence is fairly high right now, but you could be inclined to fire from the hip: not a good thing to do at the moment. Take your time and discuss things with people who are in the know.

20 FRIDAY
Moon Age Day 1 Moon Sign Pisces

This is a really good day for assessing your own position and situation in life generally. You are likely to be attentive to detail, but less inclined to dominate others with your own ideas. The more sensitive side of your nature is on display and you will appreciate the quieter aspects of life.

21 SATURDAY
Moon Age Day 2 Moon Sign Aries

Be aware that someone you know well might have some pretty startling news. There are potential gains to be made on the financial front and very few people are likely to stand in your way around this time. Concentrate your efforts with regard to a family issue and listen to what your nearest and dearest are really saying.

22 SUNDAY
Moon Age Day 3 Moon Sign Aries

Once again, you need to be on the lookout for new social contacts and to make the most of what life has to offer generally. Not everyone appears to be on your side at the moment, but when it matters the most you will be able to make some headway. Avoid getting involved in pointless rows with friends or family members.

23 MONDAY
Moon Age Day 4 Moon Sign Aries

Today should be given over to the things that most appeal to you and you won't be too concerned with the more practical aspects of life. There is the possibility of some slight financial gains, though these are likely to come along by chance rather than as a result of your own direct planning.

24 TUESDAY
Moon Age Day 5 Moon Sign Taurus

This is not a period during which you can expect to make too many gains. Take a cautious approach to most matters and be willing to have a rest. There are plenty of good trends waiting in the wings, but it is difficult for them to manifest themselves whilst the Moon is in Taurus.

25 WEDNESDAY
Moon Age Day 6 Moon Sign Taurus

Energy and enthusiasm are likely to be in short supply, but probably only for a few hours. Simply be patient and pick up a good book or watch a film. You can't get ahead in the way you would wish, but your zodiac sign can understand that there are times to move and times to stay still.

26 THURSDAY
Moon Age Day 7 Moon Sign Gemini

Now you can balance periods when you honestly want to withdraw into yourself with those times when you need to have a very positive response to others. Confidence is hard to find on occasion, but if you rely more heavily on the support that comes from your loved ones, you should manage well enough.

27 FRIDAY
Moon Age Day 8 Moon Sign Gemini

Someone or something in your daily life is definitely on your mind at the moment and you may even be quite obsessive about it. The more you deal with the minutiae of life, the less you will be concerned with a specific issue. Try to relax, even though that might be rather difficult under present trends.

28 SATURDAY
Moon Age Day 9 Moon Sign Cancer

Don't waste your time on trivialities. You should be quite keen to look at the main options life is offering, even if you are regularly interrupted by situations that are of no real importance. The end of this month shows a glimmer of optimism with regard to a job issue that has been on your mind for a while.

March

2015

YOUR MONTH AT A GLANCE

($+$) = Opportunities are around   ($-$) = Be on the defensive   = Life is pretty ordinary

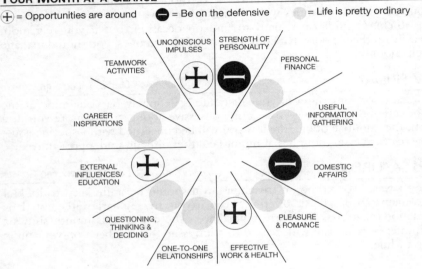

MARCH HIGHS AND LOWS

Here I show you how the rhythms of the Moon will affect you this month. Like the tide, your energies and abilities will rise and fall with its pattern. When it is above the centre line, go for it, when it is below, you should be resting.

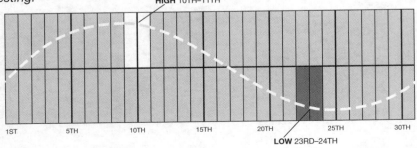

HIGH 10TH–11TH

1ST   5TH   10TH   15TH   20TH   25TH   30TH

LOW 23RD–24TH

1 SUNDAY
Moon Age Day 10 Moon Sign Cancer

You can probably make use of some pretty subtle tactics at present. When it comes to getting what you want, you can be second to none now and show a great ability to persuade others that your point of view is the right one. Don't be too quick to jump to conclusions in matters relating to love.

2 MONDAY
Moon Age Day 11 Moon Sign Leo

Not everything you want is going to turn out right, but you do have the ability to prioritise those situations in which you simply know you can succeed. Routine matters take on a slightly exciting feel and the most mundane of relationships have lots to offer today. Give yourself a break from something you hate.

3 TUESDAY
Moon Age Day 12 Moon Sign Leo

A positive focus on career developments helps to take your mind off slightly negative trends in other directions. This stage of the working week will offer you the chance to plan ahead towards a weekend that can offer significant rewards. Romance could well be highlighted by this evening.

4 WEDNESDAY
Moon Age Day 13 Moon Sign Leo

This is a time during which it will be vital to keep personal comments out of diplomatic discussions. Try not to get too hung up on details and do yourself a favour in terms of finances by taking money that is clearly being offered. Someone you haven't seen for ages could be returning to your life around now.

5 THURSDAY
Moon Age Day 14 Moon Sign Virgo

Friendship and group encounters take on a good feel and your level of co-operation is now that much greater. Once again, friends you haven't seen for some time make a return visit to your life and even general gossip is of specific interest to you right now. Plan a journey today, even if it won't take place for months.

6 FRIDAY
Moon Age Day 15 Moon Sign Virgo

You will get the best from life if you mix and mingle with as many different people are you can. Arrangements for travel or meetings could offer the odd problem, but in the main you are funny, easy to talk to and great to have around. If words of love come your way later in the day, believe what is being said.

7 SATURDAY
Moon Age Day 16 Moon Sign Libra

Your common sense cuts in now and you may decide to slow things down. You need to find the time to tell people how you are feeling and that is exactly what you can do today. Give yourself a pat on the back for a recent success, but don't get too complacent. There is plenty to be done in the days ahead.

8 SUNDAY
Moon Age Day 17 Moon Sign Libra

You should find that this is a highly social sort of Sunday that allows you to mix freely with a host of different types. Your imagination is strong and you are likely to be thinking up new schemes to pep up your life. Quieter hours could follow in the evening, when you should be pleased to put your feet up.

9 MONDAY
Moon Age Day 18 Moon Sign Libra

A quieter day can be expected because the Moon is now in your solar twelfth house. You will need to check and recheck certain matters before you commit yourself and there could be a general feeling of lethargy. Your interests are best served by socialising with trusted friends or relatives.

10 TUESDAY
Moon Age Day 19 Moon Sign Scorpio

Opportunities are coming your way that you probably didn't expect. These have a definite bearing on the lives of working Scorpios, though they may reflect to a degree on your home life, too. Any strengthening in your finances could leave you with slightly more flexibility.

11 WEDNESDAY
Moon Age Day 20 Moon Sign Scorpio

Getting a great deal done is par for the course this Wednesday. This is a good time for shopping, travelling, going out with friends and doing a host of other things that are right up your street. You value give and take in personal relationships and will be fun to have around under most circumstances.

12 THURSDAY
Moon Age Day 21 Moon Sign Sagittarius

It's clear you want to assert your ideas to others at home, but this is less easy out there in the wider world. You might have trouble getting through to types who think about life in a very different way than you do. Allowing those around you the right to be the way they naturally are is imperative, but you can't emulate them.

13 FRIDAY
Moon Age Day 22 Moon Sign Sagittarius

Find some space in between the various responsibilities of life and situations should go more smoothly for you. Time and energy can be saved if you simply let others take some of the strain. There are a few setbacks to deal with, though most of these are minor and you can sort them easily.

14 SATURDAY
Moon Age Day 23 Moon Sign Sagittarius

It will be easy to find a warm welcome wherever you go today. The weekend strengthens your social impulses and makes it almost vital for you to mix with other people. Spending long periods on your own is not to be recommended at present, and neither is backing off when things don't go your way.

15 SUNDAY
Moon Age Day 24 Moon Sign Capricorn

You have a great desire to get out and about socially. You are second to none when it comes to speaking your mind at the moment. The attitude of friends is very positive and they tend to back you up when you need it the most. A particular job that might have been quite demanding could be nearly finished.

16 MONDAY
Moon Age Day 25 Moon Sign Capricorn

There might be a slight testing of your patience today, most likely as a result of work and the way colleagues or superiors seem to be taking you for granted. It would be better not to react too strongly, but rather to show how sweet you can be. Some extra forbearance now pays dividends further down the line.

17 TUESDAY
Moon Age Day 26 Moon Sign Aquarius

There is great personal strength on display right now, together with a sort of regal quality in your nature that others notice almost immediately. Although you might think you aren't flavour of the month with certain individuals, you should soon discover that nothing could be further from the truth.

18 WEDNESDAY
Moon Age Day 27 Moon Sign Aquarius

Things generally are likely to get done quicker than you might have expected. Confidence is quite high and the planet Mars in particular gives an edge to your nature that can be very useful. There is nothing sedentary about your behaviour and Scorpio can be quite biting in discussions.

19 THURSDAY
Moon Age Day 28 Moon Sign Pisces

This is clearly a time to focus on what you want most from life. There is help around when you need it, together with newcomers to your life who can offer a different sort of way of looking at old situations. Routines won't seem too appealing and it is clear that you gain the most when overturning previous taboos.

20 FRIDAY
Moon Age Day 0 Moon Sign Pisces

If there are any frustrations at all today, these come from not being able to make everyone do what you would wish. There are certain people around who simply will not change their attitude, no matter how much you show them they are wrong. Standard responses won't work in some situations, so be original.

21 SATURDAY
Moon Age Day 1 Moon Sign Aries

Life on the whole ought to feel fairly stable today, but there is a tinge of potential excitement that simply will not go away. It might take you a while to wake up to new potential, but once you do nothing prevents you from following it. There is an almost pathological need at present to be loved and to know that you are.

22 SUNDAY
Moon Age Day 2 Moon Sign Aries

Now you could so easily find that you are in a deeply nostalgic frame of mind and will spend more time looking at the past than might be good for you. There's no real problem here unless you begin regretting anything. The only way to face is towards the future, though the lunar low will slow down the next couple of days.

23 MONDAY
Moon Age Day 3 Moon Sign Taurus

Today brings with it the lunar low. Although this can hold you back, no association of the Moon is all that bad for Scorpio because yours is a water sign. An over-emotional response now and again today is likely and you will simply have to allow yourself the right to be somewhat out of sorts.

24 TUESDAY
Moon Age Day 4 Moon Sign Taurus

It would be sensible to maintain your low profile and to wait for more favourable circumstances before trying to push forward with any specific, new project. Concern for family members could be evident, which is fairly typical for your zodiac sign at present and has little to do with the present position of the Moon.

25 WEDNESDAY
Moon Age Day 5 Moon Sign Gemini

Friends can bring a greater sense of social freedom into your life at this stage of the week. Even though there is plenty to keep you busy in a practical sense, you are bound to make time to please old pals. Don't get anxious about any issue you can't control. You find other water sign people, for example Pisceans, attractive now.

26 THURSDAY
Moon Age Day 6 Moon Sign Gemini

It looks as though you will encounter the odd or unusual quite a lot at the moment. This is no problem at all for Scorpio, because such things are meat and drink to your rather unusual nature. Try to stay away from the dark side of your mind today. It has its place, but can restrict forward movement when it really matters.

27 FRIDAY
Moon Age Day 7 Moon Sign Cancer

Emotional issues are probably dealt with a great deal more easily than you anticipated and you have what it takes to bring your partner round to a more rational point of view than the one he or she seems to be enjoying at the moment. This would be a good day for writing emails or sending important text messages.

28 SATURDAY
Moon Age Day 8 Moon Sign Cancer

You want to get ahead in some way today, but could feel yourself somewhat restricted by the less than helpful qualities of those you have to rely on. This is an enduring theme for the end of March, but if you put in that extra bit of effort you can rely on yourself more and get round potential sticking points.

29 SUNDAY
Moon Age Day 9 Moon Sign Cancer

Although there could be a few ups and downs in your personal life, Sunday as a whole ought to be quite progressive and very interesting. Get yourself out more and don't simply stick around your home. The more you socialise, the greater the incentive to get ahead in new ways.

30 MONDAY
Moon Age Day 10 Moon Sign Leo

A few minor disagreements might have to be overcome before you can get your own way today. All the same, you might be forced to ask yourself whether the end result from putting in so much effort is worth it. Only you can decide. A more romantic quality should begin to take you over by the evening.

31 TUESDAY

Moon Age Day 11   Moon Sign Leo

Revitalise your personal life whenever you can. Make sure you are first when it comes to handling out romantic compliments and put new zest into an old attachment, if you get the chance. There isn't a great deal to be achieved professionally today, so you may as well concentrate on things closer to home.

2015

Your Month at a Glance

(+) = Opportunities are around   ⊖ = Be on the defensive   ● = Life is pretty ordinary

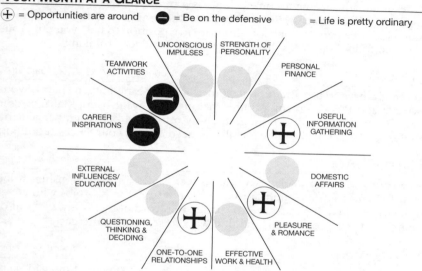

April Highs and Lows

Here I show you how the rhythms of the Moon will affect you this month. Like the tide, your energies and abilities will rise and fall with its pattern. When it is above the centre line, go for it, when it is below, you should be resting.

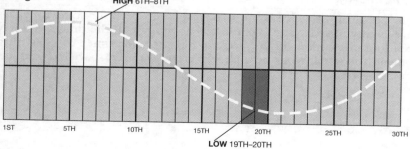

65

I WEDNESDAY
Moon Age Day 12 Moon Sign Virgo

There are likely to be a few stresses in emotional attachments at the moment. The best way to avoid these is to keep things light and open, rather than trying to have deep and meaningful conversations. There are signs that there could be slightly more cash about today than you were expecting.

2 THURSDAY
Moon Age Day 13 Moon Sign Virgo

Professional advancement comes along as a result of who rather than what you know. Keep your eyes open because there are opportunities now to impress specific people, some of whom are in a position to help you out. Your approach to life is now less likely to be clouded by deep thinking.

3 FRIDAY
Moon Age Day 14 Moon Sign Virgo

You might have to pay attention to something that is no longer a part of your own life and this can seem a bother because you want to look ahead right now. Don't be too quick to judge the way others are behaving, particularly family members. Finally, there is really no need to rush your fences at present.

4 SATURDAY
Moon Age Day 15 Moon Sign Libra

If you are a weekend worker, you can expect professional relationships to be great fun and to offer significant potential rewards. For Scorpios who are at home today, there is a real need to change to record domestically. Get out of the house if you possibly can and find ways to see issues differently.

5 SUNDAY
Moon Age Day 16 Moon Sign Libra

It is true that there are certain obstacles to be overcome and life can seem a little turbulent as a result. This should not be too much of a problem, as long as you maintain a healthy sense of humour and don't allow issues to get on top of you. There are friends on whom you can rely, most likely later in the day.

6 MONDAY
Moon Age Day 17 Moon Sign Scorpio

Your personal influence is the strongest it has been for some time. You have energy to spare and it could feel as though all the things you have been looking for are coming together at the same time. You may want to avoid too much work because it is clear you need space to breathe.

7 TUESDAY

A word in the right ear can work wonders for you now and brings you closer to achieving an objective that is very close to your heart. Spread out the responsibilities of the day and be willing to allow others to take some of the strain. It's a fair exchange, because you are making them laugh.

8 WEDNESDAY

Positive influences are more apparent than ever, even though the lunar high is starting to fade. It is your turn to shine, after a beginning to the month that was slightly less than helpful in an overall sense. There might be just a worry or two about apparently dwindling resources, but everything should turn out fine.

9 THURSDAY

There is no shortage of things to be done, but because you are adopting a new attitude you should find things falling into place quite neatly. Personal relationships are now an issue again, but in a far more positive way than appears to have sometimes been the case during the last couple of weeks.

10 FRIDAY

Now there is extra confidence and happiness showing up in your social life. New friends are likely to appear who bring with them the chance of looking at old issues in new ways. When you have set your mind on a particular course of action, don't take no for an answer.

11 SATURDAY

You could need some special help in order to get you out of a jam, though it is one that owes nothing to your own decisions or past actions. If you explain yourself to the right people, there is every reason to believe they can reverse difficult situations. Much of life is a state of mind at present.

12 SUNDAY

Looking at life through the eyes of other people has never been easier and this can prove to be a tremendous gift. Don't worry about the somewhat offhand attitude of a specific friend who is going through a hard time and could be inclined to lash out at those he or she cares for the most.

13 MONDAY
Moon Age Day 24   Moon Sign Aquarius

Social matters and teamwork situations are where your most rewarding moments arise at the beginning of this week. Someone is filled with admiration regarding the way you have dealt with a specific issue and it looks as though you are going to be number one in his or her books.

14 TUESDAY
Moon Age Day 25   Moon Sign Aquarius

The things that others are saying have a great bearing on the way you think today. Although you are not likely to become depressed at this time, you are inclined to dig deep inside that fathomless mind of yours. If this gives others the impression you are down in the dumps, you will want to reassure them this is not the case.

15 WEDNESDAY
Moon Age Day 26   Moon Sign Pisces

The things you hear now are useful in a general sense and allow you to assist the world at large. You may not have a massive bearing on society, even at a local level, but every little helps. Concern for others is always a part of what you are, but rarely more so than seems to be the case now.

16 THURSDAY
Moon Age Day 27   Moon Sign Pisces

There is a great deal to be had today through teamwork and general co-operation with others. With a lot to gain from taking on new projects, you should be quite energetic and anxious to help out when you can. Some unusual circumstances could surround aspects of your love life later in the day.

17 FRIDAY
Moon Age Day 28   Moon Sign Aries

Although probably not exactly the luckiest day of the month, things do tend to fall into place fairly well today. The difference is that what comes your way is now generally as a result of your own efforts and not restricted to chance happenings. You might be sought out for your specific expertise.

18 SATURDAY
Moon Age Day 29   Moon Sign Aries

When it comes to personal objectives, things happen today that put you fully in the picture. Watch out though, because you could be slightly accident prone and might end up doing certain jobs more than once in order to get them right. Use that good Scorpio intuition in order to work out how best to react.

19 SUNDAY
Moon Age Day 0 Moon Sign Taurus

You show yourself to be a good listener today, which is a positive way to use the lunar low period. There is time to hear exactly what other people are thinking and to do what you can to sort out their worries. Confidences will be strictly kept and most of the people you meet retain a deep confidence in you.

20 MONDAY
Moon Age Day 1 Moon Sign Taurus

You can expect a day during which you can't make the headway that has been easy of late. All you can do is show a degree of patience and take a well-earned rest instead. Don't let small irritations get in the way. The Moon might be in your opposite sign but there are other positive planets around.

21 TUESDAY
Moon Age Day 2 Moon Sign Gemini

Things are still looking pretty good in a practical sense. Attitude is important when getting on at work and you won't have things all your own way in any sphere of life. Accommodation and understanding is the key, particularly when you are dealing with younger family members who insist on being awkward.

22 WEDNESDAY
Moon Age Day 3 Moon Sign Gemini

A little daydreaming is no problem and is actually quite essential to the Scorpio nature. Don't push any issue for today, but instead be willing to watch and wait. By tomorrow everything is likely to change, so there isn't too much sense in rushing your fences for the moment. Friends should be very accommodating.

23 THURSDAY
Moon Age Day 4 Moon Sign Gemini

There are some significant bonuses around at the moment, though none of them is obvious and you will have to turn over a few stones in order to get the very most out of life generally. Strong support from friends and from specific family members should convince you to stride forward into new areas of life.

24 FRIDAY
Moon Age Day 5 Moon Sign Cancer

Your intuition is honed to perfection right now, so you should have no difficulty at all when it comes to assessing the potential in people or situations. Whatever the weather is doing at the moment, you can gain significantly from getting some fresh air and from being in stimulating and even exciting company.

25 SATURDAY
Moon Age Day 6 Moon Sign Cancer

In-depth discussions are more likely to work out positively for you today than might have been the case earlier. At the same time there is a strong romantic influence around at the moment, together with a feeling that you maybe haven't paid your partner the amount of attention he or she deserves of late.

26 SUNDAY
Moon Age Day 7 Moon Sign Leo

Messages are coming along at the moment and you need to pay attention to them. The only problem might be that they appear in the strangest places. The odd, the unusual and the downright peculiar all have a part to play in your day and conspire to make this one of the weirdest yet most fascinating periods of the month.

27 MONDAY
Moon Age Day 8 Moon Sign Leo

Busy professional trends come and go in the week ahead, leaving you with more time to get on with things that suit you personally. Although there are significant interruptions you have it within you to keep your eye on the ball. One thing you find it difficult to avoid now is gossip, which is likely to prove quite diverting.

28 TUESDAY
Moon Age Day 9 Moon Sign Leo

It isn't likely to be existing friends that stand out today so much as newcomers in your life. Scorpio people tend to have very few close friends, but a new one could definitely be made around now. All aspects related to outdoor matters, such as gardening for example, will have a real appeal at the moment.

29 WEDNESDAY
Moon Age Day 10 Moon Sign Virgo

There still isn't any trouble at all in getting your message across, even though Scorpio can sometimes go through fairly quiet periods. There are gains to be made from taking the initiative and a lot to be done in a practical sense. Scorpio is really on the ball at the moment and firing on all cylinders.

30 THURSDAY
Moon Age Day 11 Moon Sign Virgo

There are signs that this could be a fairly good day from a financial point of view. It is probably as a result of past efforts that you find things going your way right now and you could discover that you are slightly better off than you thought. Family members bring along some pleasant surprises when they are most welcome.

May

2015

YOUR MONTH AT A GLANCE

⊕ = Opportunities are around   ⊖ = Be on the defensive   ⬤ = Life is pretty ordinary

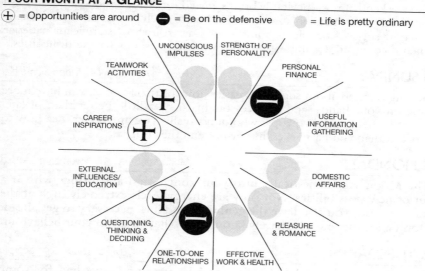

TEAMWORK ACTIVITIES

UNCONSCIOUS IMPULSES

STRENGTH OF PERSONALITY

PERSONAL FINANCE

CAREER INSPIRATIONS

USEFUL INFORMATION GATHERING

EXTERNAL INFLUENCES/ EDUCATION

DOMESTIC AFFAIRS

QUESTIONING, THINKING & DECIDING

PLEASURE & ROMANCE

ONE-TO-ONE RELATIONSHIPS

EFFECTIVE WORK & HEALTH

MAY HIGHS AND LOWS

Here I show you how the rhythms of the Moon will affect you this month. Like the tide, your energies and abilities will rise and fall with its pattern. When it is above the centre line, go for it, when it is below, you should be resting.

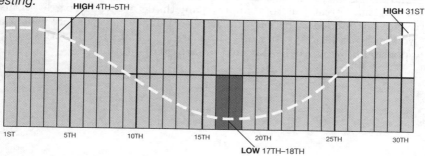

HIGH 4TH–5TH

HIGH 31ST

1ST 5TH 10TH 15TH 20TH 25TH 30TH

LOW 17TH–18TH

I FRIDAY
Moon Age Day 12 Moon Sign Libra

Ensuring that you are properly in the know regarding things that are happening around you at the moment is very important. Don't be too quick to jump to unnecessary conclusions, especially regarding the way others are behaving. Some small financial gains are possible.

2 SATURDAY
Moon Age Day 13 Moon Sign Libra

The weekend almost inevitably brings a need for change and a desire to push the pedal to the metal in a social sense. Mix as freely as you can with as many different sorts of people as come your way. You show significant patience when it comes to dealing with friends who are presently having difficulties.

3 SUNDAY
Moon Age Day 14 Moon Sign Libra

Getting out and about should be easier now for two reasons: you have more time on your hands, and finances ought to be a little better than of late. Don't be held back by people who don't really have any better idea how to proceed than you have, even if they pretend they do.

4 MONDAY
Moon Age Day 15 Moon Sign Scorpio

The Moon sails majestically into your zodiac sign and brings with it a lot of new possibilities. Not only are energy levels extremely high at the moment, but you also have the genuine good luck necessary to get ahead. Don't allow people who barely know you to have a say in your behaviour.

5 TUESDAY
Moon Age Day 16 Moon Sign Scorpio

There is the potential today for the best time you have had for some time. Your judgement is good and you feel as though you could run the world single-handedly. This isn't true, of course, but at least dealing with your small part of it ought to be child's play at the moment.

6 WEDNESDAY
Moon Age Day 17 Moon Sign Sagittarius

You can gain a great deal from simply talking things over today, partly because you are surrounded by people who are so reasonable and who are willing to give you a fair hearing. At work, there are potential gains in terms of the responsibilities you will be expected to take on in future.

7 THURSDAY

Moon Age Day 18 Moon Sign Sagittarius

It is extremely important to you at the moment that you are liked. That's fine and it is part of the person you are, but you can't expect everyone to think you are flavour of the month. Going to extremes to bring someone on side who just doesn't understand the way you tick is a waste of energy.

8 FRIDAY

Moon Age Day 19 Moon Sign Capricorn

A total change of scene would suit you down to the ground now. Even if this is not possible, you can at least ring the changes in one way or another. Those amongst you who have decided on a holiday this early in the year could have made a very sensible decision. It is a break from routine you need the most.

9 SATURDAY

Moon Age Day 20 Moon Sign Capricorn

Your ability to communicate with your partner may not be so great at present, which is why a third party might prove to be necessary. All in all, this is not going to be a bad day, but it could prove rather tedious unless you allow yourself the opportunity to break with weekend routines in some way.

10 SUNDAY

Moon Age Day 21 Moon Sign Aquarius

Everyday routines keep you nicely on the go today, though you will find once again that there is probably very little to set this day apart and you may be sometimes a little bored with the routine nature of life. The answer lies in your own hands and is down to the amount of effort you choose to put in.

11 MONDAY

Moon Age Day 22 Moon Sign Aquarius

A sort of lively sociability seems to prevail as you embark on another working week. There probably won't be anything extraordinary about today, but it does have its positive moments, not least in love. Explaining the way you feel about anything right now brings you to a better understanding of yourself.

12 TUESDAY

Moon Age Day 23 Moon Sign Aquarius

Expect a slightly low-key sort of day and one during which you may not have quite the impact on the world you would wish. The more you commit yourself to routine matters, the greater the contentment you are likely to find. Scorpio is very thoughtful at present and it shows in most of what you do.

13 WEDNESDAY
Moon Age Day 24 Moon Sign Pisces

There are matters close to you heart today that ought to be discussed with others. Getting to the bottom of a mystery is something else that appeals to you right now and your world could be filled with little puzzles of one sort or another. Attention to detail is good and allows you to score some successes.

14 THURSDAY
Moon Age Day 25 Moon Sign Pisces

If you are having personal difficulties of one sort or another, this might be the best time to sort them out. Your reasoning is sound and it isn't hard for you to explain yourself to others, particularly in an emotional sense. Getting this close to the heart of your zodiac sign is rare and a great experience for those you love.

15 FRIDAY
Moon Age Day 26 Moon Sign Aries

The most rewarding moments now come as a result of personal experiences and your attitude to love. If you are a young Scorpio or between romances, this is a time when you should be keeping your eyes open. To say that you have an admirer, secret or otherwise, is likely to be an understatement.

16 SATURDAY
Moon Age Day 27 Moon Sign Aries

Your desire to escape is born of a number of different planetary positions and influences but since this is a Saturday, you could at least indulge yourself. It doesn't matter if you only go as far as your local shopping centre. What proves to be important is that you don't lock yourself away at home this weekend.

17 SUNDAY
Moon Age Day 28 Moon Sign Taurus

Focus on practical details, especially if you are at work. You are able to enlist the support of individuals you haven't been close to before and might make one or two new friends on the way. When you are not dealing with the mundane you could find your mind wandering to some interesting and far-away places.

18 MONDAY
Moon Age Day 0 Moon Sign Taurus

Although it appears that others are getting on better than you are, this is little more than an illusion to which you are clinging. You really do need to look at matters with a longer term perspective and not get carried away by the events of any one day. Keep up your efforts to get ahead in the professional world.

19 TUESDAY ☿
Moon Age Day 1   Moon Sign Gemini

Only you can decide whether or not to believe everything you hear today. Communication can have a definitely deceptive edge and it is likely to be the case that someone is trying to take you for a ride. Any advantage you can gain in the personality stakes is to be grabbed with both hands now.

20 WEDNESDAY ☿
Moon Age Day 2   Moon Sign Gemini

You show great sympathy for the underdog today, but there is nothing very extraordinary about that – it's just the sort of person you are at present. However, this is no reason to give those around you the impression that you are some sort of sucker. There is a great potential for visiting new places now.

21 THURSDAY ☿
Moon Age Day 3   Moon Sign Cancer

This is a time during which you actively want to reach out socially and to make a good impression. You may decide to take on some new educational interest or to show the more creative qualities within your nature more than might have been possible in the recent past. A good period for new starts.

22 FRIDAY ☿
Moon Age Day 4   Moon Sign Cancer

It is likely that you find the necessary energy to break new ground effectively is missing, just when you need it the most. There are ways round this slight inconvenience, such as getting others to work on your behalf while you supervise. Someone you thought disliked you could be proving the exact opposite later today.

23 SATURDAY ☿
Moon Age Day 5   Moon Sign Leo

The weekend might just bring a few surprises and at a time when they can really pep up your life. You can't take anything for granted at the moment and should be willing to go with the flow, especially in a social sense. The better you react to changing circumstances, the greater the rewards that will come your way.

24 SUNDAY ☿
Moon Age Day 6   Moon Sign Leo

There are some points to be scored today, both at work and in a more personal sense. With plenty to play for and people quite willing in the main to follow your lead, there is no reason to hang back. Once work is out of the way you will want to turn your mind to something particularly different.

25 MONDAY ☿ *Moon Age Day 7 Moon Sign Leo*

This would be a great time to plan a trip out, even if it is only to somewhere fairly local. You are quite likely to become bored with routine at the moment and would respond very positively to a complete change. A few hours away would make all the difference and you could return raring to get going.

26 TUESDAY ☿ *Moon Age Day 8 Moon Sign Virgo*

Arguing for your limitations isn't something you are likely to be doing at all today. On the contrary you might believe you are capable of almost anything. Scorpio is now even braver than usual and that means you could take risks. Better to stick to the difficult rather than to try for the impossible.

27 WEDNESDAY ☿ *Moon Age Day 9 Moon Sign Virgo*

Getting the results you want from life, especially at work, should not prove to be very difficult today. In most matters you are on the ball and will also be in a good position to offer a little assistance to others. The odd and the unusual have a specific fascination for you at present, but there is nothing unusual about that.

28 THURSDAY ☿ *Moon Age Day 10 Moon Sign Libra*

There is a strong boost to your imagination right now and this proves to be extremely useful because in at least some cases reality is only a step beyond belief. The strength of your personality is likely to show itself under various circumstances and you seem to have what it takes now to turn heads.

29 FRIDAY ☿ *Moon Age Day 11 Moon Sign Libra*

Your energy should be well boosted today and you ought to find most things going your way. All the same, you need to show a higher degree of patience when you are dealing with family members, some of whom seem to be doing just about everything they can to prove awkward.

30 SATURDAY ☿ *Moon Age Day 12 Moon Sign Libra*

A slightly quieter phase could overtake you, if only for today. It looks as though you will be happy to spend a certain amount of time on your own and you should be rather reflective. This doesn't mean you are either glum or unhappy and it is important to let others know that you are as cheerful as ever.

31 SUNDAY   ☿

The lunar high might take you completely by surprise this time around. There you are plodding along nicely, when you discover that everything goes into hyper-drive. All the same, you will respond positively to new social possibilities and the chance to really make an impression when it matters the most.

June

2015

Your Month at a Glance

(+) = Opportunities are around   ● = Be on the defensive   ● = Life is pretty ordinary

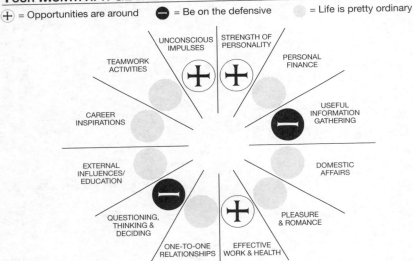

UNCONSCIOUS IMPULSES
STRENGTH OF PERSONALITY
TEAMWORK ACTIVITIES
PERSONAL FINANCE
CAREER INSPIRATIONS
USEFUL INFORMATION GATHERING
EXTERNAL INFLUENCES/ EDUCATION
DOMESTIC AFFAIRS
QUESTIONING, THINKING & DECIDING
PLEASURE & ROMANCE
ONE-TO-ONE RELATIONSHIPS
EFFECTIVE WORK & HEALTH

June Highs and Lows

Here I show you how the rhythms of the Moon will affect you this month. Like the tide, your energies and abilities will rise and fall with its pattern. When it is above the centre line, go for it, when it is below, you should be resting. **HIGH** 1ST

HIGH 27TH–29TH

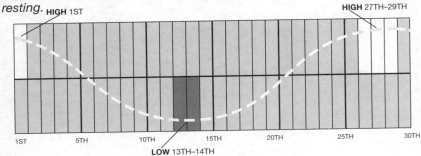

1ST   5TH   10TH   15TH   20TH   25TH   30TH

LOW 13TH–14TH

1 MONDAY *Moon Age Day 14 Moon Sign Scorpio*

What a great time this is to get new plans out in the open and working for you. Friends and relatives alike should be only too willing to lend a hand, the more so because your personality is so bubbly at present. Getting on with just about anyone proves to be as easy as pie.

2 TUESDAY *Moon Age Day 15 Moon Sign Sagittarius*

Taking yourself or in fact anyone else for granted is not to be recommended at the moment. You are likely to gloss over issues that you don't want to deal with and this could be a mistake. Analyse things carefully, in the way that Scorpio people usually do. That way nobody can be one step ahead of you.

3 WEDNESDAY *Moon Age Day 16 Moon Sign Sagittarius*

There is a degree of restlessness about at the moment and this means having to move around as freely as you can. It certainly won't be the sort of period during which you would relish being tied to the same spot or being involved in pointless routines. You would be happier travelling as much as possible.

4 THURSDAY *Moon Age Day 17 Moon Sign Sagittarius*

Love trends are on the up and you can certainly turn heads wherever you go. Whether relationships are established ones or brand new, this is the time to get it on with the main person in your life. It is difficult to hide the sensual qualities of your water sign nature at this time, no matter how hard you might try.

5 FRIDAY *Moon Age Day 18 Moon Sign Capricorn*

You are scoring significant points at present where communication is concerned. If there are jobs about that you don't like the look of, get them out of the way as early in the day as you can. Beware of some discomfort that might be caused by minor health problems, but this should diminish quickly.

6 SATURDAY *Moon Age Day 19 Moon Sign Capricorn*

Despite the fact that it may appear from time to time as though things are not really going your way today, you need to keep your eye on the future and to plan ahead. By tomorrow, more positive trends are on the way and you should be fully up to speed. Keep away from negative types and make your own decisions.

7 SUNDAY ☿ *Moon Age Day 20 Moon Sign Aquarius*

Things you have been anticipating for a while now seem to be working out the way you would wish. You have demonstrated both patience and persistence, and it shows. You are such a pleasant person at present that few will deny you your moment of glory. Those who prove awkward are not worth considering for now.

8 MONDAY ☿ *Moon Age Day 21 Moon Sign Aquarius*

When it comes to personal encounters, you might not have all it takes to make the best impression today. If, for example, you were thinking of popping the question, you should avoid doing so until at least tomorrow. Ordinary, casual encounters with friends and associates should fare somewhat better as the day progresses.

9 TUESDAY ☿ *Moon Age Day 22 Moon Sign Pisces*

The needs of today should be running fairly smoothly and your general level of good luck is certainly higher than it has been so far this month. If you feel like taking the odd chance, then go ahead. There are strong supporting trends in your solar chart that indicate a desire to have fun.

10 WEDNESDAY ☿ *Moon Age Day 23 Moon Sign Pisces*

Though your wits are sharp and your aims seem to be on target, there are areas in which you will have to show a little more care this Wednesday. You might not be exactly on top form professionally. Avoid taking risks with your career and wait to see what happens regarding new offers.

11 THURSDAY ☿ *Moon Age Day 24 Moon Sign Aries*

Bringing various changes into your personal life is going to be easier today, as you will be operating on a deeply personal level. Not everyone understands the way your mind is working at the moment, but improving communication makes it a cinch when it comes to explaining what you are presently thinking.

12 FRIDAY ☿ *Moon Age Day 25 Moon Sign Aries*

The ability to attract the good things in life has perhaps not been so strong for a while, so make the most of present trends. On the personal front, you have plenty going for you and can receive all sorts of attention, some of which you weren't even looking for. Your consideration for those around you is self-evident.

13 SATURDAY
Moon Age Day 26 Moon Sign Taurus

Put a brake on ambitions at this stage of the week. For the next two days the lunar low is going to slow you down in any case and there is really no point in fighting against the odds. Instead, do what you can to enjoy yourself and be ready by Monday, when the situation improves.

14 SUNDAY
Moon Age Day 27 Moon Sign Taurus

This really is not one of the luckiest days of the month for you. Although you can't alter the fact, you can mitigate its effect by not putting yourself in the way of too many risks. Before you volunteer for anything, ask yourself if you really should be doing so at all. Simply show a little extra care until tomorrow.

15 MONDAY
Moon Age Day 28 Moon Sign Gemini

Your persuasive powers are strong and if there is something you particularly want to do, now is the time to get cracking. Most people will gladly follow your lead now, even though you are making up your mind as you go along. The sheer magnetism of your personality is on full display.

16 TUESDAY
Moon Age Day 29 Moon Sign Gemini

You need to work hard at what you like today, because then you will perform that much better. Leave aside the jobs you don't care for, at least until tomorrow. Also, the more enjoyment you get into your life, the better you will get on with those around you. This ought to be a generally satisfying day.

17 WEDNESDAY
Moon Age Day 0 Moon Sign Cancer

A more inward-looking phase is at hand, though it probably won't last all that long. You need to be introspective now and again and can gain as a result. If there is any problem at all, it comes because those around you might think they have upset you in some way. Offer a little reassurance that this isn't the case.

18 THURSDAY
Moon Age Day 1 Moon Sign Cancer

You don't mind working extra hard for some material benefits and there are plenty of them on offer when you look around. It seems you are now more likely to throw yourself into the maelstrom that can affect certain aspects of your life and you have the great ability to bring a degree of order out of apparent chaos.

19 FRIDAY
Moon Age Day 2 Moon Sign Cancer

Focus your energies on the material side of life, even though you may want to stick to what is warm and personal. You have to be in the midst of things if you want to see success coming your way. In any case, once you get started you will be glad of the results that rapidly come your way.

20 SATURDAY
Moon Age Day 3 Moon Sign Leo

A slightly quieter day is at hand, but one that still offers a great deal if you are willing to go out and get it. You will need to plan carefully at the moment in order to make certain you don't get bogged down by details. The path ahead is far from clear, but you make progress one step at a time.

21 SUNDAY
Moon Age Day 4 Moon Sign Leo

You may be forced to relinquish something in your personal life, because it is obvious that changes are necessary. These probably won't relate to relationships, but rather to the circumstances that surround them. It is possible that someone you are not directly associated with is causing some problems.

22 MONDAY
Moon Age Day 5 Moon Sign Virgo

Getting out and about should bring you into contact with those you find stimulating, interesting and useful. This may not be a day during which you get a great deal done in a material sense, but you can have fun and after a reasonably quiet spell that's important. Your creative potential is starting to show a definite improvement.

23 TUESDAY
Moon Age Day 6 Moon Sign Virgo

You can now look forward to some highlights in terms of friendship. Present trends are such that you will not only be getting on well with existing pals, but also making some new ones, in all likelihood. Don't get caught up in discussions or arguments that are not of your making and have nothing to do with you.

24 WEDNESDAY
Moon Age Day 7 Moon Sign Virgo

For much of the time co-operative ventures look particularly good and there isn't much to stand in your way when you are sharing jobs with those around you. Unfortunately, not everyone is feeling like mucking in and you will have to deal with some fairly grumpy types, too.

25 THURSDAY
Moon Age Day 8 Moon Sign Libra

Getting together in group encounters once again suits you just fine. The weekend is not far away and you could be planning something particularly exciting. For the moment you may have to catch up with one or two jobs, but will merely be setting the scene for bigger and better things that are to come soon.

26 FRIDAY
Moon Age Day 9 Moon Sign Libra

There ought to be a brand-new focus on fresh initiatives and you can't afford to stand around and wait for life to come to you. Whilst things are so positive you should be out there getting what you want, even in the face of a little opposition. People will come round to your point of view if you give them time.

27 SATURDAY
Moon Age Day 10 Moon Sign Scorpio

Along comes a physical and mental peak, courtesy of the lunar high. This is the best time of all for taking on anything new and exciting. You actively want to show how capable you are and even display a fairly intrepid quality. This is not evident all the time, so enjoy the moment.

28 SUNDAY
Moon Age Day 11 Moon Sign Scorpio

Although the lunar high is still around, it has to be said that the argumentative side of your nature is also on display, courtesy of the present position of the planet Mars. It might sometimes be difficult for you to see things from a totally reasonable or rational point of view. This will certainly be what others think.

29 MONDAY
Moon Age Day 12 Moon Sign Scorpio

There are still good trends around and that can prove to be particularly important at the beginning of another working week. With everything to play for and people taking so much notice of you, speak out and get what you want. Nobody will accuse you of being selfish, because your zodiac sign simply isn't made that way right now.

30 TUESDAY
Moon Age Day 13 Moon Sign Sagittarius

Avoid showing the possessive side of your nature, which does surface now and again. Any form of jealousy is simply a waste of time and effort – and in any case, you may be wrong in your assumptions. There are gains to be made today, but you will have to look a little more closely to find them than has been the case recently.

2015

Your Month at a Glance

⊕ = Opportunities are around   ⊖ = Be on the defensive   ⚪ = Life is pretty ordinary

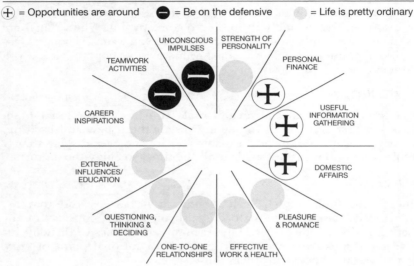

July Highs and Lows

Here I show you how the rhythms of the Moon will affect you this month. Like the tide, your energies and abilities will rise and fall with its pattern. When it is above the centre line, go for it, when it is below, you should be resting.

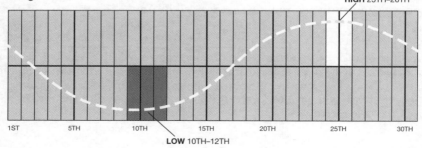

84

1 WEDNESDAY

Moon Age Day 14 Moon Sign Sagittarius

At work you have the opportunity to make great gains, particularly since you are presently willing to take the sort of chances you would have shied away from only a short time ago. The attitude of your family and friends presently makes it that much easier to gain their trust and co-operation in anything.

2 THURSDAY

Moon Age Day 15 Moon Sign Capricorn

Along comes another pretty good period relating to finances. The present position of Venus in your solar chart makes it possible for you to take a small gamble or two and to come up with the answers you would wish. Arguments should be avoided, particularly within the family.

3 FRIDAY

Moon Age Day 16 Moon Sign Capricorn

Getting what you want from others and from specific situations now appears to be that much easier. The shy and retiring side of the sign of Scorpio takes a definite holiday as you push forward with new incentives and with a confidence that others will find quite appealing.

4 SATURDAY

Moon Age Day 17 Moon Sign Aquarius

This is a period during which you can focus your mind more clearly than has been the case for several months. Although your day is likely to be extremely busy, you are able to let those around you know how important they are to you and just what their assistance in your life really means.

5 SUNDAY

Moon Age Day 18 Moon Sign Aquarius

You feel energetic and strong, which is why you could be so adventurous at present. You may even be surprised at your own tenacity and bravery, leading you to little adventures you can really enjoy. Not everyone seems to be on your side at present, though the most important people will be.

6 MONDAY

Moon Age Day 19 Moon Sign Pisces

Daily life should have plenty to keep you both occupied and interested at the beginning of a new and active week. Rules and regulations are easy to deal with; you will simply ignore them if they get in your way. Not everyone is going to be co-operative now, so stick to those who are.

7 TUESDAY
Moon Age Day 20 Moon Sign Pisces

There are some promising financial developments about and you will want to make the most of them when you can. Keep an eye open for opportunities that mean new investments, though do bear in mind that you need to think in terms of the more distant future. Romance is well starred today.

8 WEDNESDAY
Moon Age Day 21 Moon Sign Aries

Don't begin new ventures only to leave them hanging in the air. This is a time when you need to concentrate on one thing at a time and get it done before you look elsewhere. If you scatter your energies and resources, you will only find yourself repeating the same task over and over again.

9 THURSDAY
Moon Age Day 22 Moon Sign Aries

Don't miss out on any important news that is going around at present. This is a very sociable day and a time during which you will be happy to spend a few hours chewing the fat with those you know and like the best. Good fortune is likely to follow your footsteps across most of today.

10 FRIDAY
Moon Age Day 23 Moon Sign Taurus

All of a sudden, you discover reversals in fortune beginning to accumulate. Don't react too strongly to these, because they are only caused by the lunar low. In a couple of days you will be right back on form, so for the moment show some of that Scorpio patience and be willing to wait in order to gain your dreams.

11 SATURDAY
Moon Age Day 24 Moon Sign Taurus

An extra bit of effort now really counts for a great deal, which is why you are likely to be willing to march forward with determination, even though the lunar low can make this more difficult than usual. Be careful though, because you might be using more energy than would be necessary even tomorrow.

12 SUNDAY
Moon Age Day 25 Moon Sign Taurus

It is clear that you want to speak your mind on a professional matter, though this might be either difficult or impossible on a Sunday. If you are not a weekend worker, concentrate instead on things you have wanted to do in and around your home. Routine can prove to be an ally today.

13 MONDAY
Moon Age Day 26 Moon Sign Gemini

There can be a strong sense of nostalgia around at this time, leading you to spend as much time looking backwards as forwards. This contrasts markedly with your desire to get ahead and so some conflict tends to crop up within your mind today. Resolve these issues by talking about them.

14 TUESDAY
Moon Age Day 27 Moon Sign Gemini

The pursuit of practical matters offers your best chance of success so strike out rather than spending hours thinking things through. Yesterday was a time for consideration, whereas now is the moment to act. There is definite assistance around when you require it, though you might have to ask.

15 WEDNESDAY
Moon Age Day 28 Moon Sign Cancer

Halfway through the month and you still haven't done some of the things that seemed important right back at the end of June. Now is the time to assess the way situations are unfolding and to offer that extra assistance that is going to be necessary to get new plans off the drawing board and into reality.

16 THURSDAY
Moon Age Day 0 Moon Sign Cancer

Look out for special times that come like a bolt from the blue. Although the main thrust of life might seem somewhat slow, other elements can liven up your day no end simply by saying and doing the right things. What could be real pessimism at the beginning of the day might change as the hours advance.

17 FRIDAY
Moon Age Day 1 Moon Sign Leo

This is a day during which you would relish being out and about. Although not everyone is coming up trumps in terms of their general attitude, you have what it takes to cheer up the whole world if you really want to. However, in one or two specific cases you probably can't be bothered.

18 SATURDAY
Moon Age Day 2 Moon Sign Leo

Exciting social plans are coming along for many Scorpio subjects, but you might have to break out of the rat race if you want to make the very best of them. Any latent shyness in a social sense is soon blown away on a tide of enthusiasm and you could also be benefiting from better romantic possibilities.

19 SUNDAY
Moon Age Day 3 Moon Sign Leo

There is some reorganising to do, and actually the month of July is likely to be filled with it. Since you are presently in a very go-ahead frame of mind this should not be too much of a problem to you, but it does mean a busy schedule. Make sure you balance this with quiet time, possibly spent with your partner.

20 MONDAY
Moon Age Day 4 Moon Sign Virgo

There is greater backing today from the people with whom you associate the most, but professional trends might be somewhat limited for the first part of the day. With at least some hours in which to please yourself, your schedule is not quite so crowded and it ought to be possible to see the wood for the trees.

21 TUESDAY
Moon Age Day 5 Moon Sign Virgo

There should be significant support around today and a good deal of harmony when dealing with either colleagues or friends. Much is expected of you in some ways and knowing that you are being watched could make things slightly more difficult for you. Listen to what a friend is really saying and offer some timely advice.

22 WEDNESDAY
Moon Age Day 6 Moon Sign Libra

There are new developments coming along that should perk up the social scene no end. Not only are there people around who actively encourage you to make more of yourself, but you are also naturally inclined to chase positive situations. If you are about to embark on a new educational process, so much the better.

23 THURSDAY
Moon Age Day 7 Moon Sign Libra

Your imagination is stimulated by almost everything you see and do today. The world will probably have more colour and the depth of your vision knows no bounds. One implication is that you see the way forward in a very different way from someone close to you and will have to find ways to explain your thinking.

24 FRIDAY
Moon Age Day 8 Moon Sign Libra

Some objective that you have been looking at with great hope might seem to be failing now, but don't react too quickly or harshly. If you are willing to show trust in life itself, what you are seeking can still come about. There could be an important and stimulating journey in the offing soon.

25 SATURDAY
Moon Age Day 9 Moon Sign Scorpio

It might be said that luck is on your side today, but the simple fact is that you are making your own luck as you go along. Don't be shy when it comes to showing others what you are capable of achieving and do be willing to share your new views regarding work with colleagues and bosses alike.

26 SUNDAY
Moon Age Day 10 Moon Sign Scorpio

You should be able to make full use of all opportunities that come your way at present. Most spheres of your life benefit from the presence of the lunar high, but none more so than romance. Whether you have an established relationship or are just starting down the road to happiness, today offers incentives.

27 MONDAY
Moon Age Day 11 Moon Sign Sagittarius

With energy levels still running particularly high, there are people around right now who can be of specific use to you because they are racing along, too. Lady Luck should still be on your side and although Scorpio isn't give to speculating too much, you might decide to chance your arm today.

28 TUESDAY
Moon Age Day 12 Moon Sign Sagittarius

Bringing others round to your unique point of view is now likely to be easier, though you still lack a certain basic confidence in your own abilities that you can so easily telegraph to others. What really counts today is talking to the right people. Stay away from negative types who make heavy weather of everything.

29 WEDNESDAY
Moon Age Day 13 Moon Sign Capricorn

Although you won't be exactly speeding towards your objectives at this time, you will move forward slowly and steadily. Arrangements for meetings or journeys may have to be altered at the last minute and there could be a little personal frustration if your partner or sweetheart has different ideas from the ones you have.

30 THURSDAY
Moon Age Day 14 Moon Sign Capricorn

There is a new project at hand and it is one that will take all the resources you have if you are going to make the best of it. This period should also be a good in a romantic sense, and it will now be easier to find exactly the words you need to liven up your personal life more than at any time in the recent past.

31 FRIDAY
Moon Age Day 15 Moon Sign Aquarius

Some objectives fail to materialise in quite the way you had expected and you need to prepare yourself for some surprises today. The Scorpio love of luxury is really showing itself at the moment and you won't be too keen to get involved in anything dirty or messy. Lying around on a sun-lounger might appeal.

August

2015

Your Month at a Glance

⊕ = Opportunities are around   ⊖ = Be on the defensive   ⬤ = Life is pretty ordinary

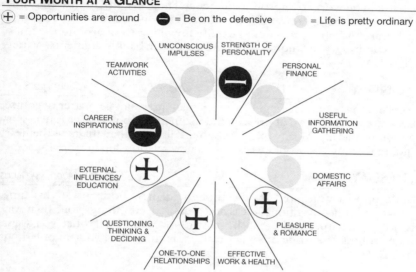

August Highs and Lows

Here I show you how the rhythms of the Moon will affect you this month. Like the tide, your energies and abilities will rise and fall with its pattern. When it is above the centre line, go for it, when it is below, you should be resting.

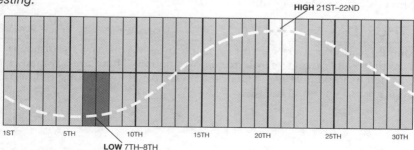

1 SATURDAY

Moon Age Day 16 Moon Sign Aquarius

As you now find yourself motivated by material issues, you should be far more willing than usual to feather your own nest. Of course, being the sort of person you are, it will be necessary for you to prove to yourself that you are helping others on the way, but that's simply your caring side showing.

2 SUNDAY

Moon Age Day 17 Moon Sign Pisces

The harder you work to improve your general financial situation at this time, the greater will be the rewards later. However, you also need excitement in your life around now and would be quite unwilling to sit around the house all day, counting your money and checking your bank statements. Variety is important.

3 MONDAY

Moon Age Day 18 Moon Sign Pisces

Success in money matters might be more than just a simple matter of course, but you are quite shrewd at present and inclined to do whatever is necessary to get on financially. Meanwhile, you should discover that affairs of the heart are going the way you would wish, with a new relationship in store for some.

4 TUESDAY

Moon Age Day 19 Moon Sign Aries

You are positively inspired by the thought of new horizons at this time, together with unconventional ideas and a desire to do things your own way. It is not your nature to be selfish, so you are able to get what you want, though without upsetting anyone on the way. In reality, your popularity is off the scale.

5 WEDNESDAY

Moon Age Day 20 Moon Sign Aries

Affairs of the heart are well accented at present and the sign of Scorpio is showing a spirited response to many aspects of life. There are signs that you might need to be careful around mechanical gadgets, one or two of which could be causing you minor problems around this time. The personal attitude of friends can be puzzling later in the day.

6 THURSDAY

Moon Age Day 21 Moon Sign Aries

Communication matters see you on top form and you have no difficulty at all getting your message across to almost anyone. There are advantages to be gained by looking at life in an unusual way. Anything curious, old or even odd is grist to your mill today.

7 FRIDAY
Moon Age Day 22 Moon Sign Taurus

You are most likely willing to forego certain pleasures around now, in order to concentrate on matters that seem particularly important on a personal level. With little room for speculation, you should hang on to your money for the moment and also shelve a few social commitments for a few days.

8 SATURDAY
Moon Age Day 23 Moon Sign Taurus

A few of the jobs you feel you must undertake today turn out to be hard work. There is no real reason why this should be the case and it might be best simply to have a rest for now. If that proves to be impossible, stick to things you like and undertake tasks one at a time for the best results.

9 SUNDAY
Moon Age Day 24 Moon Sign Gemini

There are likely to be better results from your financial efforts now, after a few days when this may not have been the case. Most of your efforts are not focused on money at the moment, though. Friendships and deeper attachments occupy your time to a much greater extent than anything else.

10 MONDAY
Moon Age Day 25 Moon Sign Gemini

In a professional sense, this is a week during which you can get things moving in a very positive way. The secret in almost any situation now is in not waiting to be asked. You are sure of yourself to a greater extent than would sometimes be the case for your zodiac sign, and others recognise this fact.

11 TUESDAY
Moon Age Day 26 Moon Sign Cancer

You will have to get one or two tedious jobs out of the way early in the day if you want longer term benefits on the social front. Be careful about investing large sums of money around now and if it is necessary for you to sign any sort of document, do so after careful thought.

12 WEDNESDAY
Moon Age Day 27 Moon Sign Cancer

You can get much from domestic matters around now, and indeed for the next three days. Caring deeply about family members, you want to do all you can to please them, even if they don't always show the degree of gratitude that would please you. Your nature is what it is: you are just plain kind now!

13 THURSDAY
Moon Age Day 28 Moon Sign Leo

You can now pursue growth in financial and professional matters more easily, though the reality of your mental processes comes slightly further down the road. Getting annoying little chores out of the way ought to prove extremely easy for you now and the tedium of life doesn't bother you in the least.

14 FRIDAY
Moon Age Day 29 Moon Sign Leo

Material and financial issues will probably prove to be more settled at this time, leading you to the feeling that you can spend more time thinking about romance and relationships generally. Do the things you really want today and not what you are expected to do. A change of heart in a personal matter is on the cards.

15 SATURDAY
Moon Age Day 0 Moon Sign Leo

Solo interests are favoured today, so this might not be quite the sociable Saturday that those around you had expected. This is not to suggest that you are isolating yourself from the world altogether. It will only take a particularly persuasive friend to drag you out on the town, where you will enjoy yourself more than you expect.

16 SUNDAY
Moon Age Day 1 Moon Sign Virgo

You should avoid any tendency towards impulse buying around now and instead conserve your money for a later time. For today, the sign of Scorpio tends to be quite capricious and inclined to shoot from the hip. This could get you into some hot water with people who are as naturally conservative as you often are.

17 MONDAY
Moon Age Day 2 Moon Sign Virgo

For now, you need to keep practical plans within the limits of what is both acceptable and possible. However, there are few limits on your personal or social life and it may well be that these are the areas of life you will want to look at most. Confidence is slightly lacking, but others do their best to support you.

18 TUESDAY
Moon Age Day 3 Moon Sign Libra

Your mind seems to dwell on the past more than would normally be the case. This is fine if you are looking for answers to present conundrums, but isn't much help if you are simply being nostalgic for its own sake. A good commitment to an idea put forward by a colleague could be the way forward.

19 WEDNESDAY
Moon Age Day 4 Moon Sign Libra

When it comes to the private side of your life you might have a few doubts and will probably have to confide in someone you trust. Not everyone is behaving in quite the way you might have come to expect and this could include your partner. Stand by a decision you have made at home, but not too forcefully.

20 THURSDAY
Moon Age Day 5 Moon Sign Libra

Don't allow yourself to become unrealistic regarding a romantic or personal matter. As the day advances, you should discover that your drive and enthusiasm are increasing and that means putting in a little more effort. Most of your hopes and wishes at the moment relate specifically to domestic and family situations.

21 FRIDAY
Moon Age Day 6 Moon Sign Scorpio

Now things change significantly and you are going to find yourself in exactly the right frame of mind to take the world by storm. There are gains to be had socially and romantically. Don't be too shy when in company and be willing to have your say. People are listening carefully.

22 SATURDAY
Moon Age Day 7 Moon Sign Scorpio

Generally speaking, you should find your level of luck extremely high at the moment. Although this won't incline you to go out and put your shirt on the horse running in the next race, you can afford to speculate a good deal more than would usually be the case. There could be some interesting compliments coming your way.

23 SUNDAY
Moon Age Day 8 Moon Sign Sagittarius

You might be slightly more forceful than you intend to be right now and need to exercise a little more self-control. Scorpio can be quite biting and even sarcastic at times and you should be aware that you can give some offence without really intending to do so. Things at home might be confusing.

24 MONDAY
Moon Age Day 9 Moon Sign Sagittarius

All the necessary components for a happy and generally successful time are now present and there will also be a great desire for travel surrounding you at the moment. Creative potential is good and this would be an excellent time to do something at home that you know will make you more comfortable later.

25 TUESDAY
Moon Age Day 10 Moon Sign Sagittarius

Keep your eyes and ears open for new information that is coming your way. Personal projects are especially well highlighted and you have what it takes to change situations to your own advantage. Love looks good, especially for those Scorpio people who are in the market for a new romance.

26 WEDNESDAY
Moon Age Day 11 Moon Sign Capricorn

You will probably have most of what you need for now on a material level, although you might be urged by others to cast your mind ahead and to plan for the distant future. This isn't an opportune time to sign documents or to make decisions that will be with you for years and years.

27 THURSDAY
Moon Age Day 12 Moon Sign Capricorn

There ought to be plenty about today that seems very rewarding. The only slight drawback could come from the fact that certain other people are not fulfilling their obligations in the way you might wish. It could be that you are expecting rather too much of them in the first place, so have a think.

28 FRIDAY
Moon Age Day 13 Moon Sign Aquarius

This may be the best day for ages with regard to romance. It is likely that your personal life has simply been jogging along of late, but there are signs that joy could be on the horizon. Something happens that makes you acutely aware of the need family members have of you at this time.

29 SATURDAY
Moon Age Day 14 Moon Sign Aquarius

In a material sense, you are now in a position to do yourself a great deal of good. This probably comes from a mixture of careful planning and in-depth discussions. Although you may also find one or two irritants troubling you throughout today, you tend to deal with them as and when they arise.

30 SUNDAY
Moon Age Day 15 Moon Sign Pisces

Communication is the way out of any jam. You are good when put on the spot now and can be more or less guaranteed to come up with the right remark. Although you might feel you are moving forward very slowly, you will be able to see your way ahead clearly. Your partner should be especially responsive.

31 MONDAY

Moon Age Day 16 Moon Sign Pisces

If there is something to celebrate at home, get stuck in and do some of the organising. You can really find joy in the success of others at this time and to do so also makes you forget some of your own cares. By the time you get back to them, at least a couple could have disappeared altogether.

September

2015

YOUR MONTH AT A GLANCE

$\oplus$ = Opportunities are around $\ominus$ = Be on the defensive   ◯ = Life is pretty ordinary

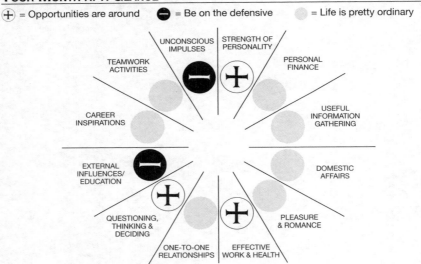

UNCONSCIOUS IMPULSES

STRENGTH OF PERSONALITY

TEAMWORK ACTIVITIES

PERSONAL FINANCE

CAREER INSPIRATIONS

USEFUL INFORMATION GATHERING

EXTERNAL INFLUENCES/ EDUCATION

DOMESTIC AFFAIRS

QUESTIONING, THINKING & DECIDING

PLEASURE & ROMANCE

ONE-TO-ONE RELATIONSHIPS

EFFECTIVE WORK & HEALTH

SEPTEMBER HIGHS AND LOWS

Here I show you how the rhythms of the Moon will affect you this month. Like the tide, your energies and abilities will rise and fall with its pattern. When it is above the centre line, go for it, when it is below, you should be resting.

HIGH 17TH–19TH

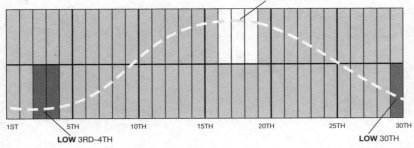

1ST   5TH   10TH   15TH   20TH   25TH   30TH

LOW 3RD–4TH

LOW 30TH

1 TUESDAY
Moon Age Day 17 Moon Sign Aries

Today should prove to be quite satisfying domestically, even if your efforts out there in the wider world are not so good. The attitude of colleagues could prove difficult to fathom, and all the more so because you seem to be doing all you can for them. At home, everyone will seem to get on well with you.

2 WEDNESDAY
Moon Age Day 18 Moon Sign Aries

Those of you who had a break last week, perhaps on holiday, will already be feeling that your rest is long over. To say you are busy at present could be something of an understatement and there won't seem to be enough hours in the day to get everything done. Remember not to rush though, because that won't help.

3 THURSDAY
Moon Age Day 19 Moon Sign Taurus

There are certain limitations around at the moment and you don't have very much choice but to accept them. The lunar low certainly won't get you down too much this time around because you have strong supporting influence, too. What might be difficult today is proving your capabilities to others.

4 FRIDAY
Moon Age Day 20 Moon Sign Taurus

It's time to slow down and take stock. If there are any jobs you really don't feel like doing today, leave them for later. Taking a well-earned break is no sin and you will work that much harder after the lunar low is gone. The attitudes of family members and friends could be difficult to fathom today.

5 SATURDAY
Moon Age Day 21 Moon Sign Gemini

If you are involved in any form of education, now is the time to really commit yourself to it. There is much to be gained in the coming months if you concentrate on what you have taken on and this applies whether or not education is part of the scenario. Friends might need special help around now.

6 SUNDAY
Moon Age Day 22 Moon Sign Gemini

At home you prove to be a natural diplomat today and can calm troubled seas generally. Some caution is necessary though, because this aspect of your nature can cause you a certain amount of aggravation. It might get tiring always being the one who solves the world's problems.

7 MONDAY
Moon Age Day 23 Moon Sign Cancer

You should be getting the best from leisure pursuits now, even if you are also very committed to your work at this time. Mixing business with pleasure should be rather easier to achieve and there is no shortage of people who want to join in and have fun with you. Concern for a younger person may be misdirected.

8 TUESDAY
Moon Age Day 24 Moon Sign Cancer

You have a real talent for getting in the good books of others today and some of the people in question really count. With infinite patience and an ability to shrug off what might sound like criticism, you are able to win through to at least a couple of important objectives before today is over.

9 WEDNESDAY
Moon Age Day 25 Moon Sign Cancer

There is an underlying element of good fortune in almost anything you undertake right now. Although not everyone seems to be on your side (a factor that is part of what this week is about), you can find enough support to get what you want. Romance is especially well starred at present.

10 THURSDAY
Moon Age Day 26 Moon Sign Leo

Family dealings and negotiations probably go well around now, so chance your arm if there is something particular you want to ask for. Friends are especially supportive and are likely to be singing your praises to the four corners of the world. Living up to expectations isn't difficult at this stage of the month.

11 FRIDAY
Moon Age Day 27 Moon Sign Leo

The most positive highlight is on domestic affairs at this stage of the week. Your relatives might feel that they have a special hold over you and could be making great demands on your time. Out there in the wider world, actions speak louder than words, a fact you understand all too well, as a rule.

12 SATURDAY
Moon Age Day 28 Moon Sign Virgo

Communication issues seem to go quite well this weekend and you won't be any sort of shrinking violet. You could easily be in the mood for shopping and will have a good nose for a bargain right now. Scorpio is sometimes quiet, but today you can haggle with the best of them.

13 SUNDAY
Moon Age Day 0 Moon Sign Virgo

You appear to be more interested in personal freedom at this time and won't stand for being fettered in any way. This is a trend that extends well into next week and the fact that you won't necessarily follow a party line is going to surprise others. It is important to explain yourself around now.

14 MONDAY
Moon Age Day 1 Moon Sign Virgo

Socially and romantically, you could find yourself being especially lucky now. Romance figures prominently in your thinking at this time, but the freedom-loving tendencies are still quite evident. What you might need most of all is a change of scene and the chance to leave routine far behind.

15 TUESDAY
Moon Age Day 2 Moon Sign Libra

The emphasis now ought to be on your creative abilities, particularly with things around the house. Making yourself feel more comfortable with your surroundings is important, especially ahead of the forthcoming winter. You may also discover that you are feeling more restless than you might have expected to be at this time.

16 WEDNESDAY
Moon Age Day 3 Moon Sign Libra

You should be able to keep up a varied and interesting schedule today, most of which comes about as a result of your own choices. Be ready to open yourself up to new situations, especially those of a social nature. At the same time, you should notice that your influence in the world at large is on the rise.

17 THURSDAY
Moon Age Day 4 Moon Sign Scorpio

This is likely to be a lucky spell for the vast majority of Scorpios. If you want you get your own slice of good fortune, you need to put yourself in the way of it. This means keeping a weather eye on what is happening around you and striking while the iron is hot. Routines are not for you today or tomorrow.

18 FRIDAY ☿
Moon Age Day 5 Moon Sign Scorpio

There is evidence that you are one of life's winners at present. With great popularity amongst almost everyone you meet, you can afford to push your luck and to ask for what you want. Even if you are refused, the fact that you were willing to speak out doesn't go without significant notice.

19 SATURDAY ☿   *Moon Age Day 6 Moon Sign Scorpio*

You are sensitive to the needs of others at the moment and easily able to put yourself in their shoes. As a result, you will be putting yourself out significantly on their behalf and can benefit from a good deal of respect as a result. The really brave side of Scorpio is likely to be on display for the next couple of days.

20 SUNDAY ☿   *Moon Age Day 7 Moon Sign Sagittarius*

Group activities would probably be a lot of fun now and you have what it takes to be at the centre of any organisation that is going on. Don't try to achieve everything all at once, but be willing to wait a little. Confidence to do the right thing remains generally strong and Sunday should be quite eventful for some of you.

21 MONDAY ☿   *Moon Age Day 8 Moon Sign Sagittarius*

Chances are you will be quite emotional today and that means you might be a little reticent about taking a chance where a particular relationship is concerned. There are financial gains to be made, even if you don't seem to have that much control over what they are and how they turn out.

22 TUESDAY ☿   *Moon Age Day 9 Moon Sign Capricorn*

Your nature is quite restless today, which means that getting out and about is very important. You are unlikely to change direction once you have made up your mind to follow a particular course of action, though you do at least need to give the impression that you are open to persuasion.

23 WEDNESDAY ☿   *Moon Age Day 10 Moon Sign Capricorn*

It looks as though you now have the necessary motivation to seek out new friends and to try experiences that haven't been a part of your life until now. There might not be anything particularly comfortable about today, but you will have plenty of enthusiasm and a desire to get where you want to go.

24 THURSDAY ☿   *Moon Age Day 11 Moon Sign Aquarius*

Although you are still generally on the ball, there are aspects of your thinking right now that others might see as being slightly irrational. The odd thing is that no matter what direction you take to gain your objectives, everything is likely to work out well for you in the end. This is not a day for undue anxiety.

25 FRIDAY ☿

Moon Age Day 12   Moon Sign Aquarius

You might just have to put up with some inconvenience today. This is likely to come from the direction of others, because certain people seem to have 'Awkward' as their middle name. Even though you are somewhat held up in terms of your own progress, you will still play the good Samaritan.

26 SATURDAY ☿

Moon Age Day 13   Moon Sign Pisces

You may find it difficult to cope if you decide to take on too many tasks at the same time today, which is why pacing yourself would be a very good idea. Remember what your strengths are and concentrate on them. Don't forget the needs of someone you don't see too often, but for whom you have the greatest regard.

27 SUNDAY ☿

Moon Age Day 14   Moon Sign Pisces

The emphasis is on work and money and you are likely to be putting in that extra bit of effort that can make all the difference. All the same, you still have a dreamy side to your nature, for which you can thank the present position of the Sun. You may need a slight nudge in order to speak your mind in a romantic sense.

28 MONDAY ☿

Moon Age Day 15   Moon Sign Aries

There is much about today that could seem quite comfortable, but at the same time little niggles do arise, mainly to do with family issues. Originality is the key to ultimate success and you will also be anxious to get things done in and around your home. Avoid unnecessary complications with friends.

29 TUESDAY ☿

Moon Age Day 16   Moon Sign Aries

The everyday running of life might be subject to bumps and grinds of one sort or another, but you will take these in your stride and will even laugh at some of the slight hiccups that come along. This is not a good time to be brooding on the past and you do need to keep your eyes firmly on the future.

30 WEDNESDAY ☿

Moon Age Day 17   Moon Sign Taurus

There are a few distractions around now, mostly of an emotional sort. It is possible that your partner is behaving rather strangely, or maybe certain family members are creating difficulties for themselves and others. None of this is likely to prevent you from being the centre of attention and attraction.

October

2015

YOUR MONTH AT A GLANCE

$\oplus$ = Opportunities are around $\ominus$ = Be on the defensive   ● = Life is pretty ordinary

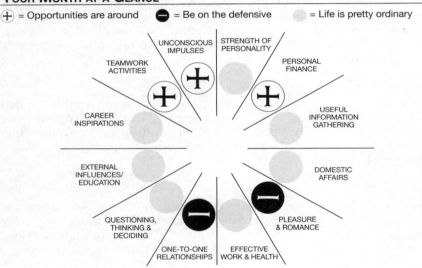

OCTOBER HIGHS AND LOWS

Here I show you how the rhythms of the Moon will affect you this month. Like the tide, your energies and abilities will rise and fall with its pattern. When it is above the centre line, go for it, when it is below, you should be resting.

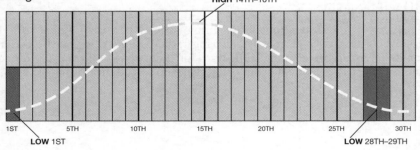

1 THURSDAY ☿ *Moon Age Day 18 Moon Sign Taurus*

There is bound to be a lull for most Scorpios around now. You shouldn't take too much notice of this fact, though it might be difficult to get things moving in a general sense. Concentrate on personal relationships, which offer more than professional or even general social trends at this time.

2 FRIDAY ☿ *Moon Age Day 19 Moon Sign Gemini*

Finances could be stronger today as you take action to consolidate a position that has been improving for a while. In addition, decisions you took some weeks or months ago are now beginning to pay dividends. Friends could be especially reliant on you at present and you will need to find the time to show them your special support.

3 SATURDAY ☿ *Moon Age Day 20 Moon Sign Gemini*

New and influential business contacts should not be overlooked at this time. This is especially true if you are self-employed or in a management position. Offers that are made outside of work may well include social gatherings that you find fascinating. Give yourself fully to new situations.

4 SUNDAY ☿ *Moon Age Day 21 Moon Sign Gemini*

Most Scorpios are footloose and fancy free today. You are in just the right frame of mind to get what you want, but you won't achieve this objective by being difficult or pushy. On the contrary, you are sweetness itself and inclined to do as many good favours as there are minutes in every hour.

5 MONDAY ☿ *Moon Age Day 22 Moon Sign Cancer*

You can gain from the presence of relatives and good friends. Associates or colleagues are not quite so fortunate to have around at this time, even though you are quite sociable and able to get on well with anyone. Routines can prove extremely tedious, which is why you need to ring the changes when you can.

6 TUESDAY ☿ *Moon Age Day 23 Moon Sign Cancer*

Although you are quite easily distracted today, you also present a very attractive picture when seen through the eyes of others. Your present slightly absentminded tendency is quite endearing and of course you can play on this fact. Getting what you want from others is not at all difficult at the moment.

7 WEDNESDAY ☿ *Moon Age Day 24 Moon Sign Leo*

Negative feelings can play an unnecessary role in your life today, which is unfortunate because they won't last long. It is very important not to react on instinct for the next day or so, but to allow nature to take its course. Long-term plans are sound and should not be ruined by spur of the moment decisions.

8 THURSDAY ☿ *Moon Age Day 25 Moon Sign Leo*

Your work can be very rewarding today and this applies every bit as much to Scorpios who are involved in full-time education or even voluntary pursuits. It is the presence of those around you that makes for such a happy time, or at least that's the way it seems to you. In reality, you are doing more than your share.

9 FRIDAY ☿ *Moon Age Day 26 Moon Sign Virgo*

You need to assert yourself in a very creative way if you are going to get the attention of people who really matter around this time. Don't hold back and be sure to speak out when you have an idea. Although prevailing trends make this slightly difficult until tomorrow, necessity demands your involvement.

10 SATURDAY ☿ *Moon Age Day 27 Moon Sign Virgo*

You need to support your actions with sensible attitudes at the moment, even if certain other people don't fully understand the way your mind is working. There are potential gains coming from a number of different directions, some of which might prove rather surprising. Relatives can be quite demanding.

11 SUNDAY ☿ *Moon Age Day 28 Moon Sign Virgo*

Material issues are inclined to work out well for you, so financial decisions can be made now with a great deal of confidence. Although you might not consider yourself to be too lucky with money as a rule, you can be at present. In terms of relationships, romance is never far from the surface now and into the new week.

12 MONDAY *Moon Age Day 29 Moon Sign Libra*

You now have a naturally affectionate nature, a fact that could hardly be lost on those with whom you deal on a day to day basis. The very warmth of your personality shines out like the morning sun today and can liven up almost anyone with whom you have contact. Continue to believe strongly in yourself.

13 TUESDAY
Moon Age Day 0 Moon Sign Libra

Because your domestic life has rarely been better than it is right now, there is a conflict of interest within you about what you should do today. On the one hand your friends are demanding your presence and attention, whilst on the other hand situations at home look warm and inviting. You will have to split your time somehow.

14 WEDNESDAY
Moon Age Day 1 Moon Sign Scorpio

You have rarely been more persuasive than you prove to be now, a real boon when it comes to getting on well in life. The lunar high is supportive of almost any venture you choose to take on and there are gains coming from a number of previously unexpected directions. Strangers can prove rewarding to have around.

15 THURSDAY
Moon Age Day 2 Moon Sign Scorpio

Your ability to get to situations before others stands you in good stead at this stage working week. This really can be a most fortunate period for you and continues to be so, even after the lunar high is gone. There are people around who want to tell you how much you mean to them.

16 FRIDAY
Moon Age Day 3 Moon Sign Scorpio

You need to involve yourself with friends or specific groups of people across today and into the future in order to achieve the greatest possible success. There are good opportunities to get ahead, even if this means being far more gregarious than would normally be the case. Attitude is everything.

17 SATURDAY
Moon Age Day 4 Moon Sign Sagittarius

By cultivating the right attitude, many of the objectives you have set yourself can be reached quicker than you expected. That doesn't mean you should rush your fences, because a little care and attention is still necessary. What you should register today is how much luck is on your side.

18 SUNDAY
Moon Age Day 5 Moon Sign Sagittarius

New plans can get off the ground, but one or two of them are going to need special help, which you need somehow to source today. A good deal of ingenuity is with you and continues to be your best guide throughout most of today. Romantic overtures could be coming from where you least expect them.

19 MONDAY
Moon Age Day 6 Moon Sign Capricorn

Beware of possible deception today, which could come from any direction. It might be that you are being misled by people who are themselves in the dark and some investigation is clearly called for. Periods of enjoyment could come from the strangest directions right now, but don't knock it!

20 TUESDAY
Moon Age Day 7 Moon Sign Capricorn

Your general position could seem weaker right now, though this is probably because you are not looking at things as positively as you might. It is important to believe in yourself and not to allow little failures to fill your mind. If things do go wrong, pick up the pieces and start again immediately.

21 WEDNESDAY
Moon Age Day 8 Moon Sign Capricorn

Love issues might seem more trouble than they are worth on occasion today, but you know in your own heart that this is not the case. If you feel as though you are taking something of a battering at the moment, turn to a good friend and laugh away your little troubles in their company. You will feel great as a result.

22 THURSDAY
Moon Age Day 9 Moon Sign Aquarius

This is a period during which you are likely to be taking the emotional side of life fairly seriously. You might be just a little too sensitive for your own good on occasions and you need to be aware of the high regard that others have for you. It's not worth taking financial risks today.

23 FRIDAY
Moon Age Day 10 Moon Sign Aquarius

You need to be where the action is, especially when it comes to the more practical side of life. If you don't get yourself involved, others will be making decisions on your behalf and that is not something you would want. In everyday life, you could be breaking rules or at the very least bending them significantly.

24 SATURDAY
Moon Age Day 11 Moon Sign Pisces

Being outdoors would stimulate you more than anything else today and the further you are from civilisation, the better you are likely to feel. A trip to the coast would suit you fine, especially if you are in the company of someone you find both interesting and quite attractive.

25 SUNDAY
Moon Age Day 12 Moon Sign Pisces

A situation created within your love life might prove to be troublesome and more than a little frustrating. Most likely this comes about because your partner or sweetheart hears what you are saying but misconstrues your meaning. It might be time to explain your point of view in a fuller and less ambiguous way.

26 MONDAY
Moon Age Day 13 Moon Sign Aries

You can make a very big impact on someone at the moment and will be quite certain about your attitude to almost anything. Positive thinking finds you in a position to overturn difficulties that were evident a few days ago and you have it within you to overcome any challenges if you've a mind to do so.

27 TUESDAY
Moon Age Day 14 Moon Sign Aries

This could turn out to be one of the most interesting parts of the month. However, the way this Tuesday actually turns out depends almost entirely on your point of view and your commitment to the moment. You have a couple of quiet days ahead of you, so it would make sense to put all your effort into today.

28 WEDNESDAY
Moon Age Day 15 Moon Sign Taurus

Communications receive a special boost and this is a time during which you can see good in just about any situation. You will need to be just a little circumspect before taking on more than you can reasonably manage. The chickens won't come home to roost for a week or two.

29 THURSDAY
Moon Age Day 16 Moon Sign Taurus

You should start to get where you want to be in a general sense and won't have too many problems persuading the world that you know what you are talking about. Silver-tongued and enchanting, you will probably be more popular at this stage of the month than has been the case for weeks.

30 FRIDAY
Moon Age Day 17 Moon Sign Gemini

Daily matters not only keep you happily on the go, but also contain much interesting information. Virtually nothing passes you by right now and you can make a silk purse out of a sow's ear. You might have a secret admirer, which although gratifying in one way could be embarrassing in another.

31 SATURDAY

Though ambitions remain strong at the moment, you really need to look at life's finer details. Attitude is very important when approaching others and especially so if you want to get them on your side. You can progress quite well, but the fact that this is the weekend might get in the way somewhat.

November 2015

YOUR MONTH AT A GLANCE

⊕ = Opportunities are around   ⊖ = Be on the defensive   ◯ = Life is pretty ordinary

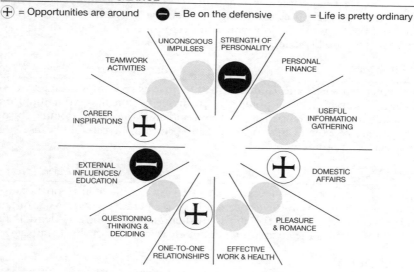

- UNCONSCIOUS IMPULSES
- STRENGTH OF PERSONALITY ⊖
- TEAMWORK ACTIVITIES
- PERSONAL FINANCE
- CAREER INSPIRATIONS ⊕
- USEFUL INFORMATION GATHERING
- EXTERNAL INFLUENCES/ EDUCATION ⊖
- DOMESTIC AFFAIRS ⊕
- QUESTIONING, THINKING & DECIDING
- PLEASURE & ROMANCE
- ONE-TO-ONE RELATIONSHIPS ⊕
- EFFECTIVE WORK & HEALTH

NOVEMBER HIGHS AND LOWS

Here I show you how the rhythms of the Moon will affect you this month. Like the tide, your energies and abilities will rise and fall with its pattern. When it is above the centre line, go for it, when it is below, you should be resting.

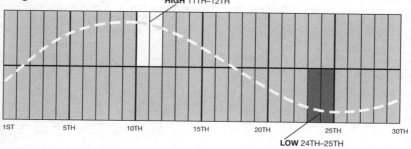

HIGH 11TH–12TH

1ST   5TH   10TH   15TH   20TH   25TH   30TH

LOW 24TH–25TH

1 SUNDAY
Moon Age Day 19 Moon Sign Cancer

Personal relationships are definitely your forte at present. Don't be put off forming a new attachment just because of what someone else says. There is a distinct possibility that any negative opinion is at least partly the result of some sort of jealousy. Don't be afraid to speak your mind today.

2 MONDAY
Moon Age Day 20 Moon Sign Cancer

Try to adopt a totally freewheeling attitude towards life right now. There appears to be no real pressure being put upon you and there ought to be plenty of time to get those jobs you don't care for done and out of the way. Some Scorpios are behaving as if it is still the weekend.

3 TUESDAY
Moon Age Day 21 Moon Sign Leo

Involvement in social and romantic matters proves to be rewarding around this time. From a practical point of view, it seems you have your mind on one task, your heart wrapped around a second and your hands doing a third. Only you are capable of this sort of juggling act, but be careful because you can't keep it up indefinitely.

4 WEDNESDAY
Moon Age Day 22 Moon Sign Leo

Teamwork is the key to success today. This isn't difficult for you because you know only too well how to get on in a co-operative sense. What might surprise you is the way a specific individual is now willing to lend their support to ventures they were quite definitely opposed to a short time ago.

5 THURSDAY
Moon Age Day 23 Moon Sign Leo

Your vitality and natural charm should make you popular with just about everybody today. As a result, it isn't difficult to get what you want from life or to persuade others that you know what you are talking about. Routines are not your cup of tea for the moment, so ring the changes whenever you can.

6 FRIDAY
Moon Age Day 24 Moon Sign Virgo

You need to use your intuition where love and relationships are concerned. Maybe your partner is not behaving as you have come to expect or else the object of your devotion still isn't noticing. There's more than one way to skin a cat and when it comes to being slightly devious you are not afraid of these tactics at the moment.

7 SATURDAY
Moon Age Day 25 Moon Sign Virgo

Although you may not be a weekend worker, trends surrounding work are at their very best today. This means that although you may not be committing yourself professionally, it is highly likely you will be planning for the future. You also show a strong tendency to move around a good deal during this Saturday.

8 SUNDAY
Moon Age Day 26 Moon Sign Libra

You are willing to make contact with almost anyone who crosses your path today. Rarely has Scorpio been more sociable and this fact shows in all your activities. This is a time to say what you think at work, in the almost certain knowledge that people who hold important positions are listening to you.

9 MONDAY
Moon Age Day 27 Moon Sign Libra

Love relationships should be working out very nicely for you and the planetary trends that cause this state of affairs act in a timely way, cropping up as they do early in the week. You are able to tell your lover how you are feeling and should expect a very definite sort of response.

10 TUESDAY
Moon Age Day 28 Moon Sign Libra

There is a possibility that you could be somewhat nervy today. If so, put this down to the present position of the Moon, just ahead of the lunar high. There is a great time in store, but for the moment you should probably stay as quiet and settled as you can and not take too many chances.

11 WEDNESDAY
Moon Age Day 29 Moon Sign Scorpio

Your physical strength now becomes much more apparent and you have a burning desire to make this time your own. No wonder! The Moon is in your zodiac sign, whilst other aspects are doing their best to add extra spice to your personal life. Be definite in your approach and employ a little cheek.

12 THURSDAY
Moon Age Day 0 Moon Sign Scorpio

Follow your intuition wherever it takes you, which could be quite a long way. Despite the fact that the best of the weather is gone for this year, you will be quite anxious to get out of the house and to move around freely. Scorpio is particularly inclined towards sports of almost any kind today.

13 FRIDAY
Moon Age Day 1 Moon Sign Sagittarius

Group involvements cause you to feel tense and you definitely need to avoid getting into situations of conflict with people who would represent formidable opponents. In any case, this really isn't your style right now, because you can get what you want by showing the pleasant side of your nature.

14 SATURDAY
Moon Age Day 2 Moon Sign Sagittarius

Partnerships and the way you relate to others generally are both interesting and important today. Any sort of business connection is especially well starred, which would be good for Scorpio subjects who are self-employed. Money could be coming your way from a fairly unexpected direction.

15 SUNDAY
Moon Age Day 3 Moon Sign Sagittarius

There is a great deal going on today that you should find to be distinctly interesting, particularly where your home life is concerned. Although there are also tasks you find distinctly tedious, you discover ways and means of getting through these without getting more upset than necessary.

16 MONDAY
Moon Age Day 4 Moon Sign Capricorn

This is a time when it would be best simply to buckle down and get on with some work. You can achieve a great deal, but not without putting in the necessary effort. Comfort and security mean little or nothing to you for much of this week. You can easily tackle several different jobs at the same time.

17 TUESDAY
Moon Age Day 5 Moon Sign Capricorn

You show a very pleasant disposition to the world at large, and even though you are so busy you will find the time to make those around you happy. They in turn will take significant notice of you and listen very carefully to those Scorpio ideas. You instinctively know what looks and feels right around now.

18 WEDNESDAY
Moon Age Day 6 Moon Sign Aquarius

You nearly always enjoy attending to the needs of others, but never more so than seems to be the case right now. However, you need to take as well as give, so don't get too embarrassed if someone wants to make a big fuss of you. Avoid jealousy where your partner or someone you really fancy is concerned.

19 THURSDAY
Moon Age Day 7 Moon Sign Aquarius

Your interests are best served today by being involved with group activities. At the moment you are a very good team player, though don't be in the least surprised if the rest of the team look to you for advice. Routines are for the birds and you tend to make up most things as you go along.

20 FRIDAY
Moon Age Day 8 Moon Sign Pisces

Avoid confrontations that are brought about as a result of your ego, which is extremely well starred at the moment. You have what it takes to continue your present successful phase, but won't do so well if you insist on falling out over details. Let others have their say and then make up your mind.

21 SATURDAY
Moon Age Day 9 Moon Sign Pisces

You need to concentrate today if you really want to get on, but if you are not at work the picture will look significantly different. Social trends are also good and you continue to turn heads when it matters. An outing of some sort this evening might suit you down to the ground, especially if you're with good friends.

22 SUNDAY
Moon Age Day 10 Moon Sign Aries

The potential for making money is still around, but unfortunately so is the likelihood of losing it. It's all a matter of balance and you can't afford to gamble as much as you have been doing. Although you are willing to stand up for yourself at this time, it is possible that you will be going a little too far.

23 MONDAY
Moon Age Day 11 Moon Sign Aries

Financial matters may seem slightly rosier today mainly because you are being more careful, but also because you are luckier again. Romance is likely to be on your mind and you could discover that you have a secret admirer. Whether or not this realisation pleases you remains to be seen.

24 TUESDAY
Moon Age Day 12 Moon Sign Taurus

Ambitions have to be shelved, though certainly not abandoned. If obstacles do make themselves obvious today, you can be quite certain that they are little more than phantoms in the night. Simply watch and wait. Your moment for advancement is likely to come much sooner than you expect.

25 WEDNESDAY *Moon Age Day 13 Moon Sign Taurus*

There are a few obstacles in your path today and there doesn't seem to be much you can do about it. If you want to enjoy the best sort of day, keep out of the limelight and simply do things that please you. Major responsibilities should probably be left until another time.

26 THURSDAY *Moon Age Day 14 Moon Sign Gemini*

Your thinking is sharp and your hunches are likely to be spot on in most situations. The only area of life in which you have to exhibit a little care is on the domestic front. It could be that your nearest and dearest don't have quite the regard for your opinions that they once had, or at least it seems that way.

27 FRIDAY *Moon Age Day 15 Moon Sign Gemini*

Today could be rather less than satisfying at home, especially if you fail to take into account the opinions of those with whom you live. All in all, it might be better to spend some time away from home. Maybe a pre-Christmas shopping spree would take your fancy or a journey to a place of great interest.

28 SATURDAY *Moon Age Day 16 Moon Sign Cancer*

You benefit from being demonstrative in a love relationship and you are still showing a strongly extroverted attitude generally. Money matters are likely to be fairly positive, though you might have to put something by with Christmas now being so close. There are definite gains to be made in terms of simple friendship.

29 SUNDAY *Moon Age Day 17 Moon Sign Cancer*

You should see financial issues on a continuing upswing. This is not only a time to build successfully on previous efforts, but also a period during which you can afford to back your most recent hunches. Gains come from some fairly unexpected places, such as junk shops or market stalls.

30 MONDAY *Moon Age Day 18 Moon Sign Cancer*

You are much more effective today than might seem to be the case, which is why you sometimes have to stand back and look at the way things are going. Although you are efficient and swift, there is really no race and it is quite important to enjoy the journey as well as the destination around this time.

December

2015

Your Month at a Glance

(+) = Opportunities are around   ⊖ = Be on the defensive   ⬤ = Life is pretty ordinary

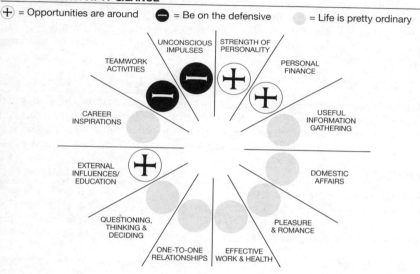

December Highs and Lows

Here I show you how the rhythms of the Moon will affect you this month. Like the tide, your energies and abilities will rise and fall with its pattern. When it is above the centre line, go for it, when it is below, you should be resting.

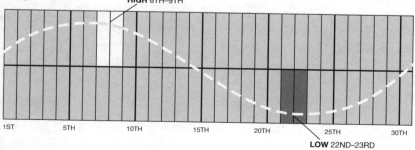

HIGH 8TH–9TH

LOW 22ND–23RD

1ST   5TH   10TH   15TH   20TH   25TH   30TH

1 TUESDAY
Moon Age Day 19 Moon Sign Leo

You show a very generous spirit today, no matter what you are doing. This increases your general popularity and ensures you of plenty of friends. There is nothing new about your behaviour at present. Probably the only difference is that others are now paying more attention than usual.

2 WEDNESDAY
Moon Age Day 20 Moon Sign Leo

Broadening your horizons is very important now. At the same time you show a strong sense of culture and a refined taste. Don't be too quick to judge either the attitude or the sensibilities of others. All in all, this can be a very useful day, but it is just possible you might be accused of being slightly snooty.

3 THURSDAY
Moon Age Day 21 Moon Sign Virgo

Although some practical issues need thinking about carefully, in a personal sense it appears that the day is your own. Not only is romance well accented at present, but common friendships can become much more with the passing of time. Don't be surprised if someone singles you out for special treatment.

4 FRIDAY
Moon Age Day 22 Moon Sign Virgo

With Christmas only a stone's throw away, now is the time to take yourself off on a shopping spree. You may or may not start out in the right frame of mind, but it won't take you long to get into the mood. Spend as much time as you can in the company of friends who have the ability to make you laugh.

5 SATURDAY
Moon Age Day 23 Moon Sign Libra

It is better to be on the move this weekend and to travel as much as you can. You are clearly curious about the world right now and keen to see as much of it as possible. If there are any restrictions placed upon you in a general sense at the moment, these probably exist more in your head than in reality.

6 SUNDAY
Moon Age Day 24 Moon Sign Libra

Prepare to make the most of the security you are feeling in your relationships as Christmas approaches. This is a very special time of year as far as you are concerned and you like to have everything as organised and comfortable as proves to be possible.

7 MONDAY
Moon Age Day 25 Moon Sign Libra

This is a quieter time, it's true, but all that's going to change very quickly with the lunar high starting tomorrow. There are times later in the day when you will have to be fully on your mettle and during which you will be called upon to make split-second decisions. This shakes you out of any lethargy.

8 TUESDAY
Moon Age Day 26 Moon Sign Scorpio

Now you are really in gear and your lunar-high focus is almost certainly going to be on Christmas. There are many practical things to be done and even if you have been very organised you will find more. Dashing about from pillar to post is definitely no problem as far as you are concerned.

9 WEDNESDAY
Moon Age Day 27 Moon Sign Scorpio

Personal ambitions and hopes can turn out pretty much the way you would expect and you show a very optimistic face to the world at large. Popularity is more or less assured and you make a very good impression, even on strangers. There are gains to be made on the financial front – perhaps you'll come across some special bargains.

10 THURSDAY
Moon Age Day 28 Moon Sign Sagittarius

Happiness through personal attachments and romance is not exactly assured around now, but it is very likely indeed. Hang on to any extra money that comes your way today, because the chances are you are going to need it. Standing by a decision you made some days ago might not be easy, but proves to be necessary.

11 FRIDAY
Moon Age Day 0 Moon Sign Sagittarius

Pay attention to detail at work if you want to ensure that everything works out the way you want. This is very important just now in a personal and a practical sense. Almost nobody wants to rain on your parade deliberately, but a friend might put his or her foot in things without realising. The result should be some laughs.

12 SATURDAY
Moon Age Day 1 Moon Sign Sagittarius

There seems to be a great deal of ego and assertiveness around at the moment and at least some of it is coming from your direction. You could be looking towards a period of very hard work in the near future and it won't help if you cause problems with the people who can best help you. A little humility now goes a long way.

13 SUNDAY
Moon Age Day 2 Moon Sign Capricorn

Consider the rights of others today and make sure that these are not being drowned by your own sensibilities. Are you really seeing things from their point of view or just kidding yourself that this is the case? A little deep thinking is called for, even if there are interruptions practically all day long.

14 MONDAY
Moon Age Day 3 Moon Sign Capricorn

Under the present trends that surround you, you might have to be slightly more frugal than you have been expecting. Perhaps you haven't got everything you need for Christmas yet, whilst at the same time money is short. With a little careful planning you can do what is necessary in terms of gifts whilst spending little and also having fun.

15 TUESDAY
Moon Age Day 4 Moon Sign Aquarius

You are very generous at the moment and that's a good thing, not least of all because you tend to get back much more than you give in one way or another. This would be a good time to enter competitions and to test your skill against others. Social trends are particularly interesting and remain so for some time.

16 WEDNESDAY
Moon Age Day 5 Moon Sign Aquarius

With the accent now firmly on enjoyable communication, you are really looking forward to what Christmas has to offer. For many of you the festive season starts right now and you will be getting into the right frame of mind. Keep an eye on a family member who might have been out of sorts recently.

17 THURSDAY
Moon Age Day 6 Moon Sign Pisces

You seem to have lots of ideas at your disposal. Even if eight out of ten of them are not workable, that still leaves two that are worth pursuing. With only a few days left until Christmas, your mind tends to travel back to previous times. There may be lessons to be learned from the past, but probably not many.

18 FRIDAY
Moon Age Day 7 Moon Sign Pisces

A friendly word in the right ear might make it easy for you to settle a personal issue that has been on your mind. At the same time you can be of significant assistance to colleagues, friends and even your partner. Scorpio is presently at its most co-operative, which enhances your natural popularity.

19 SATURDAY
Moon Age Day 8 Moon Sign Aries

There is now a good chance to improve your mind in some way, as well as to learn that you are in any case smarter than you might have thought. You love to pit your wits against those of interesting people, demonstrating a distinctly competitive edge to your Scorpio nature.

20 SUNDAY
Moon Age Day 9 Moon Sign Aries

Daily life might be subject to sudden changes and that could mean having to think on your feet a good deal today. Although you will still be comfortable at home, it's possible you will be taking some time out to visit relatives and the change of scenery could work to your advantage.

21 MONDAY
Moon Age Day 10 Moon Sign Aries

There are signs that money prospects could continue to improve as a new week gets underway. The big day is not far off, so you are likely to be working as hard as ever to ensure that everyone has a really good time. Don't get tied up in red tape, particularly at work. A clear horizon is very important around now.

22 TUESDAY
Moon Age Day 11 Moon Sign Taurus

There is a general lull around and one that could have a bearing on the way you view the end of the year. The lunar low doesn't exactly prevent you from enjoying yourself, but it can slow down your reaction time and your need for too much fun. What is most apparent today is how thoughtful you are.

23 WEDNESDAY
Moon Age Day 12 Moon Sign Taurus

You want more physical comforts right now and will be enlisting the support of loved ones in order to make certain this is possible. Luxury appeals and you won't want to be putting yourself out any more than is strictly necessary. Because you are so lovable, it is likely that you receive all the attention you desire.

24 THURSDAY
Moon Age Day 13 Moon Sign Gemini

Dashing about all the time is no way to enjoy fully what Christmas Eve has to offer you. There need to be moments during the day in which you can simply stand and look, both at your handiwork and at the world at large. This is particularly true if you have small children whose attitude to Christmas you can share.

25 FRIDAY
Moon Age Day 14 Moon Sign Gemini

Despite the fact that you enjoy the family side of Christmas, there is nothing wrong with relishing a romantic twosome. This should be a generally happy day and one that leads you to a better understanding of the way someone close to you ticks.

26 SATURDAY
Moon Age Day 15 Moon Sign Cancer

There may be some very hopeful news with regard to personal concerns and wishes on this Boxing Day. From a social and romantic point of view, it is those things that come like a bolt from the blue that presently offer the most, so don't be either upset or worried if you have to change your mind at the last minute.

27 SUNDAY
Moon Age Day 16 Moon Sign Cancer

Unexpected domestic challenges could come along at any time now. You will be expected to sort them out, which won't be easy if there are also disagreements to be dealt with. Scorpio needs to be especially patient at the moment and to show a very loving face to relatives and friends alike.

28 MONDAY
Moon Age Day 17 Moon Sign Leo

A plan of action is essential in what is likely to be a very competitive world right now. You do have a winning instinct and a desire to get ahead, but not everyone will either like or respect the methods you are using to get where you want to be. Some careful explanations may be necessary in certain cases.

29 TUESDAY
Moon Age Day 18 Moon Sign Leo

This is a good time during which to try your hand at money making and innovative enterprises. Help with these is certain if you ask around and people generally seem to want to assist you today. There is a quieter side to your nature that shows later, but in the main you are happy to be in the social mainstream.

30 WEDNESDAY
Moon Age Day 19 Moon Sign Virgo

Family gatherings ought to be of real interest now and you will be doing more than most to make these possible. Even if you do not come from a very close family background you are likely to feel more attached than usual. A sense of place and belonging is extremely important to you at present.

31 THURSDAY

Moon Age Day 20 Moon Sign Virgo

You appear to be on great form today and you could be experiencing new insights into a subject that is currently uppermost in your mind. Not everyone seems to be on the same wavelength, but by the end of the day you have plenty of energy and can really enjoy what New Year gatherings have to offer.

How to Calculate Your Rising Sign

Most astrologers agree that, next to the Sun Sign, the most important influence on any person is the Rising Sign at the time of their birth. The Rising Sign represents the astrological sign that was rising over the eastern horizon when each and every one of us came into the world. It is sometimes also called the Ascendant.

Let us suppose, for example, that you were born with the Sun in the zodiac sign of Libra. This would bestow certain characteristics on you that are likely to be shared by all other Librans. However, a Libran with Aries Rising would show a very different attitude towards life, and of course relationships, than a Libran with Pisces Rising.

For these reasons, this book shows how your zodiac Rising Sign has a bearing on all the possible positions of the Sun at birth. Simply look through the Aries table opposite.

As long as you know your approximate time of birth the graph will show you how to discover your Rising Sign.

Look across the top of the graph of your zodiac sign to find your date of birth, and down the side for your birth time (I have used Greenwich Mean Time). Where they cross is your Rising Sign. Don't forget to subtract an hour (or two) if appropriate for Summer Time.

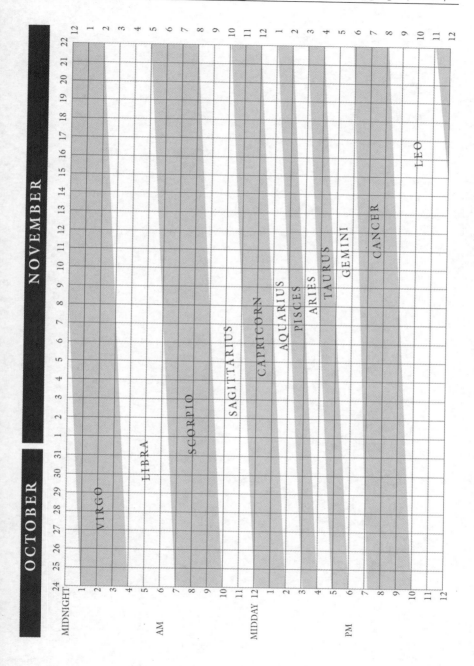

OCTOBER   NOVEMBER

VIRGO

LIBRA

SCORPIO

SAGITTARIUS

CAPRICORN

AQUARIUS

PISCES

ARIES

TAURUS

GEMINI

CANCER

LEO

THE ZODIAC, PLANETS AND CORRESPONDENCES

The Earth revolves around the Sun once every calendar year, so when viewed from Earth the Sun appears in a different part of the sky as the year progresses. In astrology, these parts of the sky are divided into the signs of the zodiac and this means that the signs are organised in a circle. The circle begins with Aries and ends with Pisces.

Taking the zodiac sign as a starting point, astrologers then work with all the positions of planets, stars and many other factors to calculate horoscopes and birth charts and tell us what the stars have in store for us.

The table below shows the planets and Elements for each of the signs of the zodiac. Each sign belongs to one of the four Elements: Fire, Air, Earth or Water. Fire signs are creative and enthusiastic; Air signs are mentally active and thoughtful; Earth signs are constructive and practical; Water signs are emotional and have strong feelings.

It also shows the metals and gemstones associated with, or corresponding with, each sign. The correspondence is made when a metal or stone possesses properties that are held in common with a particular sign of the zodiac.

Finally, the table shows the opposite of each star sign – this is the opposite sign in the astrological circle.

Placed	Sign	Symbol	Element	Planet	Metal	Stone	Opposite
1	Aries	Ram	Fire	Mars	Iron	Bloodstone	Libra
2	Taurus	Bull	Earth	Venus	Copper	Sapphire	Scorpio
3	Gemini	Twins	Air	Mercury	Mercury	Tiger's Eye	Sagittarius
4	Cancer	Crab	Water	Moon	Silver	Pearl	Capricorn
5	Leo	Lion	Fire	Sun	Gold	Ruby	Aquarius
6	Virgo	Maiden	Earth	Mercury	Mercury	Sardonyx	Pisces
7	Libra	Scales	Air	Venus	Copper	Sapphire	Aries
8	Scorpio	Scorpion	Water	Pluto	Plutonium	Jasper	Taurus
9	Sagittarius	Archer	Fire	Jupiter	Tin	Topaz	Gemini
10	Capricorn	Goat	Earth	Saturn	Lead	Black Onyx	Cancer
11	Aquarius	Waterbearer	Air	Uranus	Uranium	Amethyst	Leo
12	Pisces	Fishes	Water	Neptune	Tin	Moonstone	Virgo